180 DAYS™
Phonics
for Second Grade

T0357841

boat

soap

goat

Author
Kaitlin Blicharz, M.Ed.

Consultant

Lisa Hollis, M.A.Ed.
First Grade Teacher
Sylvan Union School District

Publishing Credits

Corinne Burton, M.A.Ed., *President and Publisher*
Gabe Thibodeau, *Content Director*
Véronique Bos, *VP of Creative*
Lynette Ordoñez, *Content Manager*
Hilary Wolcott, M.A.Ed., *Editor*
Jill Malcolm, *Senior Graphic Designer*

Standards

© Copyright 2010 National Governors Association Center for Best Practices and Council of Chief State School Officers. All rights reserved.
© Copyright 2007–2024 Texas Education Agency (TEA). All Rights Reserved.
© 2024 TESOL International Association
© 2024 Board of Regents of the University of Wisconsin System

Image Credits: all other images from iStock and/or Shutterstock

A division of Teacher Created Materials
5482 Argosy Avenue
Huntington Beach, CA 92649-1039
www.tcmpub.com/shell-education
ISBN 978-1-0876-6257-2
© 2025 Shell Educational Publishing, Inc.
Printed by: 51497
Printed in: China

Table of Contents

Introduction

180 Days of Practice

Appendix

What Is Phonics?

Learning to read is a complex process. Students must know the speech sounds associated with written letters in words, how to put those sounds together to form pronounceable words, and how to recognize words rapidly (Beck and Beck 2013). Phonics is a method of instruction that teaches learners the relationship between sounds and letters and how to use those sounds and letters to read and spell. Practice is especially important to help early readers recognize words rapidly. *180 Days™: Phonics* offers teachers and parents a full page of targeted phonics practice activities for each day of the school year.

The Science of Reading

Phonics instruction has historically been at the forefront of much debate and research. The "whole-language" approach presented in the *Dick and Jane* books dominated beginning reading instruction with its "look-say" method that required students to memorize whole words without paying any attention to decoding (sounding out) words. This method was highly criticized by Rudolf Flesch's 1955 publication *Why Johnny Can't Read* and by Jeanne Chall's 1967 publication *Learning to Read: The Great Debate*. Both researchers indicated the need for direct phonics instruction in place of teaching trial and error and the memorization of whole words. In 1997, Congress commissioned a review of this reading research. The National Reading Panel (NRP) released their report in 2000, which became the backbone of the Science of Reading. The panel's findings clearly showed that for students to become better readers, they need systematic and explicit instruction in these five areas:

- Phonemic Awareness: understanding and manipulating individual speech sounds
- Phonics: matching sounds to letters for use in reading and spelling
- Fluency: reading connected text accurately and smoothly
- Vocabulary: knowing the meanings of words in speech and in print
- Reading Comprehension: understanding what is read

An effective reading program must include instruction in foundational skills, such as phonemic awareness, as well as direct instruction in relating sounds to written letters or sequences of letters that represent those sounds.

Phonics will more than likely continue to play a key role in the Science of Reading. Decades of research have proven it to be the most effective means for building foundational literacy in learners.

What Is Phonics? *(cont.)*

Elements of Instruction

The alphabetic principle is the idea that letters and letter patterns represent the sounds of spoken language. When students who are learning to read and write begin to connect letters (graphemes) with their sounds (phonemes), they have cracked the alphabetic principle. The goal of phonics instruction is to teach students that there are systematic and predictable relationships between written letters and spoken sounds. Learning these predictable relationships helps students apply the alphabetic principle to both familiar and unfamiliar words and to begin to read with fluency.

Children use their prior learning as a bridge to new learning. For this reason, the best phonics instruction presents skills sequentially from simple to complex. According to Robert Marzano, "Practice has always been, and always will be, a necessary ingredient to learning procedural knowledge at a level at which students execute it independently" (2010, 83). Practice is especially important to help students apply phonics concepts to a wide range of words. Learners need multiple opportunities to review learned skills and to practice the relationship between letters and sound patterns.

Research to Practice

180 Days™: Phonics has been informed by reading research. This series provides opportunities for students to practice the skills that are proven to contribute to reading growth.

- Phonics concepts are presented from **simple to complex**, with prior learning embedded within each week. This provides students with **multiple opportunities to practice** target skills.

- Daily practices intentionally build upon one another to help students **bridge new learning** to prior concepts.

- Specific **language comprehension** and **word-recognition skills** are reinforced throughout the activities.

- An overview page is provided before each week to introduce key concepts and provide **explicit instructional strategies**.

- Students read and write words with target concepts to reinforce the connection between **graphemes** and **phonemes**.

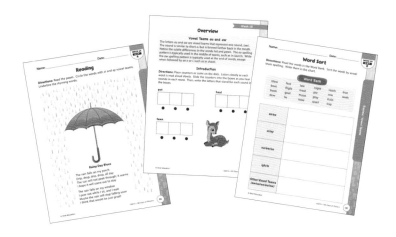

How to Use This Resource

Unit Structure Overview

This resource is divided into 36 weekly units. Each week focuses on a specific phonics concept. This provides ample practice with each pattern before moving on to more complex patterns.

Week	Phonics Pattern	Week	Phonics Pattern
Week 1	Consonants and Short Vowels	Week 19	Review: Vowel Teams
Week 2	Hard and Soft Sounds (*g, c*)	Week 20	Diphthongs *oi, oy*
Week 3	Consonant Digraphs (*ch, sh, th, wh, ph*)	Week 21	Diphthongs *ou, ow*
Week 4	Silent Letters (*wr–, –mb, –lf, kn–, –lk*)	Week 22	*R*-Controlled Vowels
Week 5	*S* Blends (*sc, sk, sm, sn, sp, st, sw*)	Week 23	Vowel-*R* Combinations *–air, –are*
Week 6	*L* Blends (*bl, cl, fl, gl, pl, sl*)	Week 24	Vowel-*R* Combinations *–eer, –ear*
Week 7	*R* Blends (*br, cr, dr, fr, gr, pr, tr*)	Week 25	Vowel-*R* Combinations *–our, –ore, –ure*
Week 8	Three-Letter Blends and Consonant Digraph Blends (*scr, spl, spr, squ, str, thr, shr*)	Week 26	Inflectional Endings *–s, –es, –ies*
Week 9	Final Consonant Blends (*–ft, –st, –lp, –nt, –nd, –mp*)	Week 27	Inflectional Ending *–ing*
Week 10	Closed-Syllable Exceptions (*all, ind, ild, old, ost, olt, ull*)	Week 28	Inflectional Ending *–ed*
Week 11	Long Vowels with Silent *E*	Week 29	Syllable Patterns VC/CV and VCCCV
Week 12	*Y* as Long *I and Long E*	Week 30	Syllable Patterns V/CV and VC/V
Week 13	Vowel Teams *ee, ea*	Week 31	Consonant +*le*
Week 14	Vowel Teams *ai, ay*	Week 32	Prefixes *un–, im–*
Week 15	Vowel Teams *oa, ow, oe*	Week 33	Prefixes *re–, dis–*
Week 16	Vowel Teams *igh, ie*	Week 34	Suffix *–ly*
Week 17	Vowel Teams *ew, ue, oo*	Week 35	Contractions
Week 18	Vowel Teams *au, aw*	Week 36	Cumulative Review

How to Use This Resource *(cont.)*

Overview Pages

Each unit follows a consistent format for ease of use. An overview page introduces phonics concepts at the beginning of each unit. These pages support family understanding and provide opportunities to prepare students for the activities presented in the following practice pages. Teachers may wish to send the page home with students at the beginning of each unit to inform parents of what is being learned at school.

A box at the top of each page explains the phonics concept presented in that week.

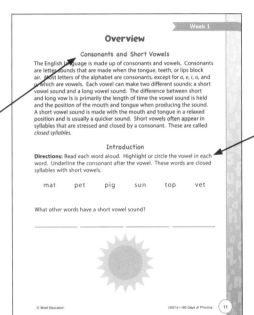

The Introduction activity provides an example of a strategy used within the unit or addresses common misconceptions with a specific phonics skill. Complete this activity as a class or in small groups to help prepare students for the upcoming topics.

How to Use This Resource (cont.)

Student Practice Pages

Practice pages reinforce grade-level phonics skills. This book provides one practice page for each day of the school year. Each day's phonics activity is provided as a full practice page, making it easy to prepare and implement as part of a morning routine, at the beginning of each phonics lesson, or as homework.

Day 1 of each week teaches students the phonics focus of the week and how to identify the target sounds.

Students practice target concepts through word play activities on **Day 3**.

At the end of the week on **Day 5**, students write words, sentences, or paragraphs containing the target concept.

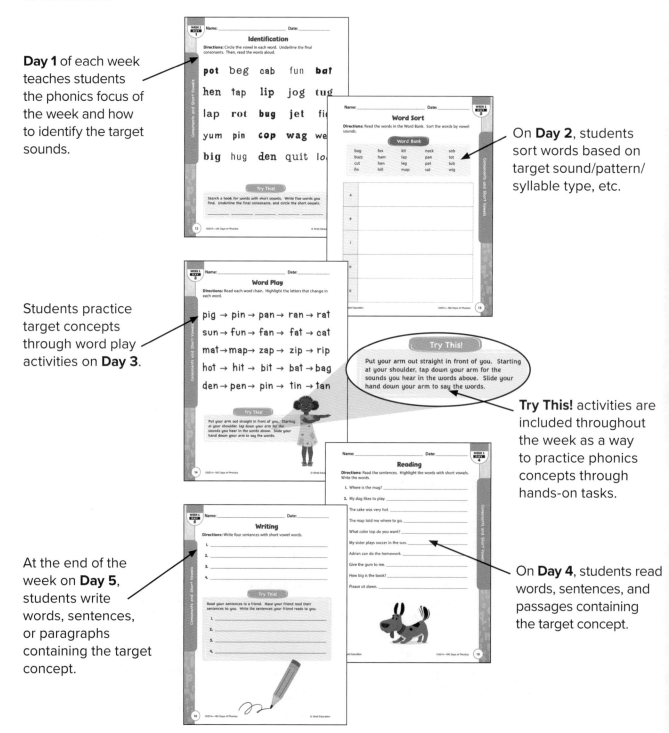

On **Day 2**, students sort words based on target sound/pattern/syllable type, etc.

Try This! activities are included throughout the week as a way to practice phonics concepts through hands-on tasks.

On **Day 4**, students read words, sentences, and passages containing the target concept.

How to Use This Resource *(cont.)*

Digital Resources

Several phonics resources are provided digitally. (See page 240 for instructions on how to download these pages.) These tools include the following:

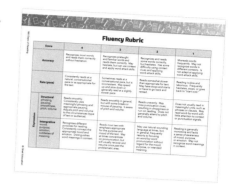

- **Standards Correlations**—This resource shows how the activities align with key standards.

- **Class and Individual Analysis Sheets**—These analysis sheets can be used weekly to track student progress toward mastery of concepts. Results can be analyzed to determine next steps for differentiating instruction to meet varying student needs.

- **Fluency Rubric**—This tool can help you assess reading proficiency and track student progress.

Instructional Options

180 Days™: Phonics is a flexible resource that can be used in various instructional settings for different purposes.

- Use the practice pages as daily warm-up activities.

- Work with students in small groups, allowing them to focus on specific skills. This setting also lends itself to partner and group discussions about the phonics focus.

- Practice pages in this resource can be completed independently during center times and as activities for early finishers.

How to Use This Resource (cont.)

Diagnostic Assessment

The practice pages in this book can be used as diagnostic assessments. These activity pages require students to identify specific phonics concepts within words, read connected text, and write responses using target concepts. (An answer key for the practice pages is provided starting on page 229.)

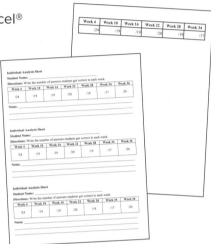

Analysis sheets are provided as Microsoft Word® and Microsoft Excel® files in the digital resources. There is a Class Analysis Sheet and an Individual Analysis Sheet. Use the file that matches your assessment needs. At the end of each week, count the number of problems students got correct on Day 4 and enter it into the chart. Depending on the type of activity, you may wish to see how many target words students identify or assess how they read the isolated words. Analyze the data on the analysis sheet to determine instructional focuses for your child or class.

The diagnostic analysis tools included in the digital resources allow for quick evaluation and ongoing monitoring of student work. See at a glance which phonics concepts students may need to explore further to develop fluency.

Using the Results to Differentiate Instruction

Once results are gathered and analyzed, use the data to determine how to differentiate instruction. The data can help determine which concepts are the most difficult for students, as well as identify students who need additional instructional support and continued practice.

The results of the diagnostic analysis may show that an entire class is struggling with a particular phonics concept. If these concepts have been taught in the past, this indicates that further instruction or reteaching is necessary. If these concepts have not yet been taught, this data is a great preassessment tool that demonstrates students do not have a working knowledge of the concepts.

The results of the diagnostic analysis may also show that an individual or small group of students is struggling with a particular concept or group of concepts. Consider pulling aside these students to instruct further on the concept(s) while others work independently. You can also use the results to help identify individuals or groups of proficient students who are ready for enrichment or above-grade-level instruction. These students may benefit from independent learning contracts or more challenging activities.

Overview

Consonants and Short Vowels

The English language is made up of consonants and vowels. Consonants are letter sounds that are made when the tongue, teeth, or lips block air. Most letters of the alphabet are consonants, except for *a*, *e*, *i*, *o*, and *u*, which are vowels. Each vowel can make two different sounds: a short vowel sound and a long vowel sound. The difference between short and long vowels is primarily the length of time the vowel sound is held and the position of the mouth and tongue when producing the sound. A short vowel sound is made with the mouth and tongue in a relaxed position, and is usually a quicker sound. Short vowels often appear in syllables that are stressed and closed by a consonant. These are called *closed syllables.*

Introduction

Directions: Read each word aloud. These words are closed syllables with short vowels. Highlight or circle the vowel in each word. Underline the consonant after the vowel.

mat   pet   pig   sun   top

What other words have a short vowel sound?

_____ _____ _____ _____

Name: _____   Date: _____

Identification

Directions: Circle the vowel in each word. Underline the final consonant.
Then, read the words aloud.

Consonants and Short Vowels

pot	beg	cab	fun	**bat**
hen	tap	**lip**	jog	tug
lap	rot	**bug**	jet	fig
yum	pin	**cop**	**wag**	web
big	hug	**den**	tip	log

Try This!

Search a book for words with short vowels. Write five words you
find. Underline the final consonants, and circle the short vowels.

_____ _____ _____ _____ _____

Word Sort

Directions: Read the words in the Word Bank. Sort the words by vowel sounds.

Word Bank

hen	fin	sat	neck	hill
pan	tub	buzz	sob	tot
cut	mop	fox	leg	bug
kit	wig	pet	ham	lap

a	
e	
i	
o	
u	

Consonants and Short Vowels

Name: _____ Date: _____

Word Play

Directions: Read each word chain. Highlight or circle the letters that change in each word.

Consonants and Short Vowels

pig → pin → pan → ran → rat

sun → fun → fan → fat → cat

mat → map → zap → zip → rip

hot → hit → bit → bat → bag

den → pen → pin → tin → tan

Try This!

Put your arm out straight in front of you. Starting at your shoulder, tap down your arm for the sounds you hear in the words above. Slide your hand down your arm to say the words.

Reading

Directions: Read the sentences. Highlight or circle the words with short vowels. Write the words.

I. Where is the mug? _____

2. My dog likes to play. _____

3. The cake was very hot. _____

4. The map told me where to go. _____

5. What color top do you want? _____

6. My sister plays soccer in the sun. _____

7. Adrian can do the homework. _____

8. Give the gum to me. _____

9. How big is the book? _____

10. Please sit down. _____

Consonants and Short Vowels

Name: _____ Date: _____

Writing

Directions: Write four sentences with short-vowel words. Be sure each sentence begins with a capital letter and ends with a punctuation mark.

1. _____

2. _____

3. _____

4. _____

Try This!

Read your sentences to a friend. Have your friend read their sentences to you. Write the sentences your friend reads to you.

1. _____

2. _____

3. _____

4. _____

Consonants and Short Vowels

Overview

Hard and Soft Sounds

g, c

Some consonants have more than one sound. Consonants *g* and *c* have hard and soft sounds. Consonant *g* has a hard /g/ sound in words such as *grape* and *grand*. But it has a soft /j/ sound in words such as *gem* and *giraffe*. Consonant *c* has the hard /k/ sound in the words *cape* and *coin*. But it has the soft /s/ sound in the words *cell* and *citrus*. The sounds for *c* and *g* are soft when followed by *i, e,* or *y*.

Introduction

Directions: Listen as the words below are read aloud. Then, follow the steps.

cent	cut	city	gym	gum

1. Underline the beginning consonant in each word.

2. Highlight or circle the vowel that comes after the beginning consonant. Vowels *i, e,* or *y* follow each soft sound.

3. Read the words aloud. Listen for the hard and soft sounds. Noticing which vowels come after *g* and *c* can help you know which sound to use.

Name: _____ Date: _____

Identification

Directions: Read the words in the Word Bank. Circle the words with soft sounds. Box the words with hard sounds. Write the words next to the matching pictures.

Word Bank

cap	cent	cereal	cot	gab	game	gel	gem

1.  _____

2.  _____

3. _____

4. _____

5.  _____

6.  _____

7.  _____

8.  _____

Word Sort

Directions: Read the words in the Word Bank. Sort the words by consonant sounds. Write them in the chart.

Word Bank

cab	cell	cop	gem	got
can	cent	gap	gent	gym

soft c	
hard c	
soft g	
hard g	

Hard and Soft Sounds

Try This!

Look around the room. Find two other things that have soft consonant sounds in their names. Write the names of the objects in the correct rows above.

Name: _____ Date: _____

Word Play

Directions: Choose four words from the previous page. Write them on the lines. Slide counters or coins into the boxes for the sounds in the words. Read the words aloud.

1. _____

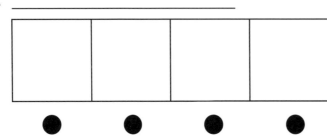

2. _____

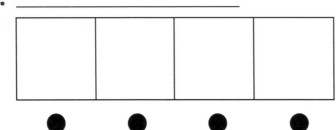

3. _____

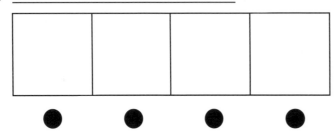

4. _____

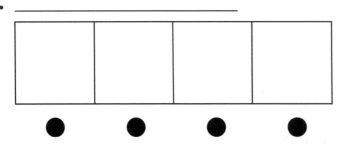

Try This!

Make a word chain. Start with the word *gem*. Change one sound at a time. Write your new words.

gem

_____

_____

_____

_____

_____

Name: _____   Date: _____

Reading

Directions: Read the sentences. Circle words with soft consonant sounds. Write the words you circle.

1. Can I have some ice in my drink? _____

2. Maria found a gem in her toy box. _____

3. She had rice with her dinner. _____

4. I have one cent in my pocket. _____

5. My cell phone rang and rang. _____

6. Wash your hands so you do not spread germs. _____

7. Put the gel in the drawer. _____

8. I like to run and jump in gym class. _____

Name: _____   Date: _____

Writing

Directions: Use the words in the Word Bank to complete the sentences.

Hard and Soft Sounds

Word Bank

cells	city	gem
cent	gel	gym

1. I put _____ in my hair.

2. My mom will go to the _____ after school.

3. I found a _____ in my jewelry box.

4. I like to visit the big _____.

5. A penny is one _____.

6. Bees store honey in the _____ of the hive.

Try This!

Choose four words from the Word Bank. Write two sentences using two of the words in each sentence.

1. _____

2. _____

Overview

Consonant Digraphs

ch, sh, th, wh, ph

Consonant digraphs are two or more consonants that work together to create one sound. For example, the consonants *p* and *h* form the digraph *ph*, which can represent the /f/ sound, such as in *phone*. The most common digraphs that beginning readers need to recognize are *ch*, *sh*, *th*, *wh*, and *ph*. Beginning readers often read these letters as individual sounds.

Introduction

Directions: Place a counter or coin on each dot. Listen as the first word below is read aloud slowly. Slide the counters into the boxes as you hear the sounds in the word. Repeat this for each word.

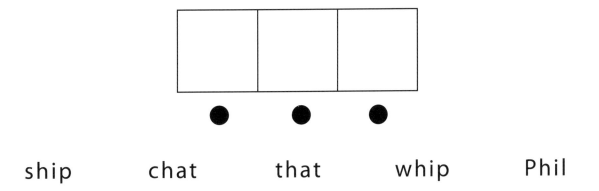

| ship | chat | that | whip | Phil |

The first two letters in each of the words above are digraphs. The two letters make one sound.

130214—180 Days™: Phonics

Name: _____ Date: _____

Identification

Directions: Read the words aloud. Draw sound boxes around the sounds in each word.

Example: thin

1. c h i p

2. r i c h

3. s h i p

4. m a s h

5. t h i c k

6. m a t h

7. w h e n

8. w h i c h

9. P h i l

10. g r a p h

Try This!

Choose five words. Read each word to a friend. Have your friend tap the sounds in the words. Then, switch roles.

Word Sort

Directions: Read the words in the Word Bank. Sort the words by consonant digraph sounds. Write them in the chart.

Word Bank

shell	graph	wish	chop
chess	than	Ralph	whip
think	chunk	wham	shock

/ch/	
/sh/	
/th/	
/wh/	
/ph/	

Word Play

Directions: Read the words. Change the consonant digraphs to make new words. Then, choose three words, and write sentences with them.

Consonant Digraphs

1. **ch**ip → [ ] ip

2. **sh**in → [ ] in

3. wi**th** → wi [ ]

4. **ch**op → [ ] op

5. ma**sh** → ma [ ]

6. **th**at → [ ] at

7. ba**th** → ba [ ]

8. **ch**ick → [ ] ick

9. **th**en → [ ] en

10. **wh**am → [ ] am

Sentences

1. _____

2. _____

3. _____

Reading

Name: _____   **Date:** _____

Directions: Read the sentences. Highlight or circle words with consonant digraphs. Some sentences have more than one. Write these words.

1. The little chick can jump. _____

2. The soft, red shell was in the hot sand. _____

3. Can you chop it up? _____

4. Thank you for the big gift! _____

5. My dad and Gram will chit and chat. _____

6. Which friend will play chess? _____

7. Phil will try his best in class. _____

8. I can play tag with my friends at recess. _____

9. How much is that toy? _____

10. I must take a bath before bed. _____

Try This!

Practice writing the highlighted words in sand, shaving cream, or rice. Say the sounds as you write the words.

Consonant Digraphs

Name: _____   Date: _____

Writing

Directions: Write the words from the Word Bank in alphabetical order. Then, choose three words and write them in sentences. Be sure each sentence begins with a capital letter and ends with a punctuation mark.

Word Bank

which	chick	graph
shell	think	rich

Consonant Digraphs

Alphabetical Order

1. _____

2. _____

3. _____

4. _____

5. _____

6. _____

Sentences

1. _____

2. _____

3. _____

Overview

Silent Letters

wr–, –mb, –lf, kn–, –lk

Silent letters appear as a pair of letters in which only one letter makes its typical sound. A silent letter in a word is written but not pronounced, such as the /l/ in *chalk*. The most common silent-letter combinations beginning readers need to learn are *wr–, –mb, –lf, kn–,* and *–lk*. This chart shows the sounds represented by these silent-letter combinations.

Letter Combination	Represented Sound	Silent Letter(s)	Example
wr–	/r/	*w*	wrap
–mb	/m/	*b*	lamb
–lf	/f/	*l*	calf
kn–	/n/	*k*	knot
–lk	/k/	*l*	walk

Introduction

Directions: Listen as each word below is read aloud slowly. Some of the letters cannot be heard. Underline the silent letters in the words. The first one has been done for you.

k̲not   half   chalk   wrong   thumb

Name: _____   Date: _____

Identification

Directions: Read the words. Circle the words with silent letters.

wrap	thick	**knit**	kiss	sing
math	**thumb**	**gem**	**yell**	when
sock	**wrong**	**chess**	**with**	numb
shell	half	**cell**	chess	**gym**
knob	pink	wreck	stem	**calf**
shop	wham	**chalk**	wash	**thing**

Try This!

Use clay to make four small balls. Read one of the words above to a friend. Have your friend squish a ball of clay for each sound they hear. Then, switch roles.

Word Sort

Directions: Read the words in the Word Bank. Sort the words by their silent-letter spellings. Write them in the chart.

Word Bank

numb	talk	wrong	knit	chalk
wreck	knob	calf	thumb	knot

wr–	
–mb	
–lf	
kn–	
–lk	

Silent Letters

Name: _____ Date: _____

Word Play

Directions: Read the words in the Word Bank. Underline the silent letters. Write the words next to the matching pictures.

Word Bank

calf	knit	talk	wrap
half	lamb	thumb	write

Silent Letters

1. _____

2.  _____

3.  _____

4.  _____

5.  _____

6. 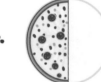 _____

7. _____

8. _____

Reading

Directions: Read the passage. Highlight or circle the words with silent letters. Then, write the words on the lines.

Helpful Jobs

What do you want to be when you grow up? You can be many things! Some jobs help people. A doctor helps people get better. A teacher helps children learn. A firefighter keeps people safe. These jobs are important because they help us.

A doctor can help if you are sick or hurt. They can tell you what is wrong. If you get in a wreck, they will help you heal. They may wrap a broken limb or numb any pain. Doctors keep us well and happy.

A teacher can help you learn and grow. They have a knack for learning! They know how to do math, read, and write. They ask you questions and help you get the answers. With the help of a teacher, you can be a whiz kid!

A firefighter can help in your community. If you have an emergency, you can call them. They will talk to you and figure out what to do. Do not forget to thank them!

Many jobs can help people. What will you do?

Words

_____ _____ _____ _____

_____ _____ _____ _____

Silent Letters

Name: _____   Date: _____

Writing

Directions: Read the words in the Word Bank. Choose five words, and write them in sentences.

Word Bank

calf	half	knot	talk	wreck
chalk	knock	lamb	thumb	wrong

Silent Letters

1. _____

2. _____

3. _____

4. _____

5. _____

Try This!

Play a game of charades with friends. Act out a word from the Word Bank. Have your friends guess which word you act out. Then, switch roles.

Overview

S Blends

sc, sk, sm, sn, sp, st, sw

Consonant blends are two or more consonants that appear before or after a vowel. The consonant sounds blend quickly, but they retain their sounds. For example, there are four sounds in the word *snap*: /s/ /n/ /ă/ /p/. But you read the *s* and *n* quickly together so that they make a smooth sound. This week, students will learn about seven common consonant blends with the letter *s*.

Introduction

Directions: Listen as each word below is read aloud slowly. Follow the steps.

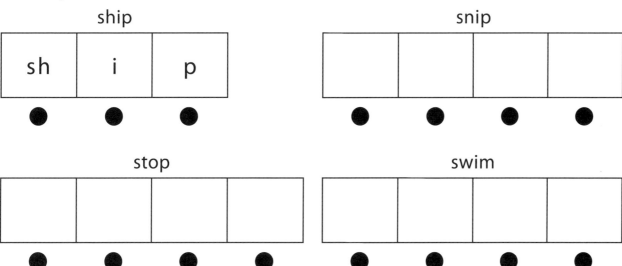

1. Place counters or coins on the dots below each box.
2. Slide the counters into the boxes as you hear the sounds in the word *ship*.
3. Slide the counters as you listen to the word *snip*. Notice that the word *ship* has three sounds, and the word *snip* has four sounds. *Snip* has an *s* blend. You blend the *s* and the *n*, but you can still hear each sound.
4. Slide the counters as you listen to the words *stop* and *swim*.
5. Write the letters that stand for each sound in the boxes. The first one has been done for you.

Name: _____   Date: _____

Identification

Directions: Read the words. Underline the letters that make the consonant blends.

S Blends

scuff	step	**swing**	scan	snack
spin	stuck	**swam**	**smell**	skin
snap	**stick**	**scuff**	swim	stuff
speck	swat	**scab**	snug	**stop**
skid	smog	smock	sway	**stack**

Try This!

Practice segmenting sounds using sound boxes. Place counters or coins on the dots. Slide the counters into the boxes as you say the sounds in the words above.

Word Sort

Directions: Read the words in the Word Bank. Sort the words by *s* blends. Write them in the chart.

Word Bank

scab	snug	sped	scuff
stub	skin	skill	sniff
swing	skip	smog	spill
scan	smell	snap	still

sc–	
sk–	
sm–	
sn–	
sp–	
st–	
sw–	

Try This!

Write each word from the Word Bank on a note card. Place the note cards around the room. Ask a friend to find the words. Read the words, and sort them a different way.

Name: _____   Date: _____

Word Play

Directions: Read the words in the Word Bank. Highlight or circle the words in the word search.

X	M	P	V	S	K	I	N	B	E
K	V	G	S	S	W	V	C	D	S
S	V	S	I	T	S	I	V	J	T
M	S	C	Y	E	N	L	N	Y	O
E	T	U	W	M	A	E	Z	G	P
L	I	F	Z	Q	C	U	E	M	Y
L	F	F	C	K	K	U	M	N	W
B	F	U	B	H	Y	U	R	D	N
S	K	I	L	L	E	O	B	J	Y
T	S	T	U	C	K	J	O	X	S

Word Bank

scuff	skin	snack	stiff	stuck
skill	smell	stem	stop	swing

Reading

Directions: Read the letter. Circle the words with *s* blends. There are 10 different words.

Dear Jonah,

My teacher, Mr. Smith, says we will write to the kids at another class. He says that it is a good way to get to know others. I am happy that you are my pen pal! I want to hear all about your class, friends, and things you like to do.

My favorite time of day is when we go to the gym. In the gym, we can run, skip, and play. When the weather is good, we go outside and play games. It takes a lot of skill to be a good athlete. I always try my best!

I also really like recess. I swing with my friends, and we talk about many things. My best friend, Steph, likes to sniff the flowers by the playground. She brings them to our teacher. Mr. Smith sticks all of them in a cup with water and puts them on his desk. They make the classroom smell great!

These are just a few things I like to do. I will write you again to tell you more! I look forward to your letter.

From,
Trish

Name: _____ Date: _____

S Blends

Writing

Directions: Use the words in the Word Bank to complete the sentences.

Word Bank

| skunk | spell | stack | stop | swim |
| smell | spin | stem | stuff | swing |

1. The trash can is full and has a bad _____.

2. The _____ of the flower is tall.

3. I found a _____ under my deck.

4. The best thing to do on the playground is _____.

5. I need to pack my _____ for the trip.

6. Please _____ the books on the top shelf.

7. Can you _____ these words?

8. Miguel will _____ the dreidel with his family.

9. Please _____ at the shop on the way home.

10. The ducks _____ up the river.

Try This!

Write a story using some of the words in the Word Bank. Read your story to a friend.

Overview

L Blends

bl, cl, fl, gl, pl, sl

Consonant blends are two or more consonants that appear before or after a vowel. With *L* blends, the consonant sounds blend quickly, but they retain their sounds. For example, there are four sounds in the word *clap*: /c/ /l/ /ă/ /p/. But the *c* and the *l* are read quickly to make a smooth sound. This week, students will learn about six common *L* blends.

Introduction

Directions: Listen as each word below is read aloud. Tap the table for each sound you hear in the words. The beginning sound in each word blends with the consonant *L*. Cover the words. Then, write each word as you listen to the words again.

click	plum	black	slip	glad

1. _____

2. _____

3. _____

4. _____

5. _____

Name: _____ Date: _____

Identification

Directions: Read the words. Circle the words with *L* blends.

L Blends

class	which	**bath**	glad	stub
flock	glass	**floss**	clink	chick
blend	cloth	**sloth**	slug	wink
snack	jazz	**skate**	chest	map
plank	flash	chunk	smell	**flag**
plum	bank	slack	swing	stack

Try This!

Use letter tiles or magnets to build words with *L* blends. Write five of them.

_____ _____ _____ _____ _____

© Shell Education

Word Sort

Directions: Read the words in the Word Bank. Sort the words by consonant blends. Write them in the chart.

Word Bank

class	flesh	stop	pluck
smog	scuff	gloss	plum
clock	fluff	glum	smell
swam	glad	stick	snap

S Blends	
L Blends	

Try This!

Write the words in the Word Bank on note cards. Sort the words differently. Get creative!

L Blends

Name: _____ Date: _____

Word Play

Directions: Write the *L* blend at the beginning of each set of letters. Read the words you made. The first one has been done for you.

bl–	*cl–*	*fl–*
bl ank	_____ am	_____ ip
_____ ip	_____ iff	_____ uff
_____ ob	_____ uck	_____ ash
_____ ink	_____ oth	_____ oss

gl–	*pl–*	*sl–*
_____ am	_____ um	_____ ug
_____ ad	_____ ank	_____ ick
_____ oss	_____ uck	_____ oth
_____ ug	_____ an	_____ ing

Try This!

Fold a sheet of paper in half horizontally. Then, fold it into thirds vertically. You will have six boxes. Write the six *L* blends you have learned about at the top of each box. Then, draw pictures of words that have each blend.

Reading

Directions: Read the sentences. Highlight or circle words with *L* blends.
Some sentences have more than one. Write these words.

1. Can you pull the sled up the tall hill?_____

2. There is a flag in every classroom. _____

3. The camera flash lit up the room. _____

4. Josh slammed the ball into the net! _____

5. I am glad you did your best on the quiz. _____

6. Maria will watch the clock for class to end. _____

7. Please plug in the phone. _____

8. The slush made it hard to walk. _____

9. The glass will crack if you are not careful. _____

10. Plan to floss at bedtime. _____

L Blends

Name: _____ Date: _____

Writing

Directions: Write four sentences with words that have *L* blends. Be sure each sentence begins with a capital letter and ends with a punctuation mark.

1. _____

2. _____

3. _____

4. _____

Try This!

Read your sentences to a friend. Have your friend read their sentences to you. Write the sentences your friend reads to you.

1. _____

2. _____

3. _____

4. _____

Overview

R Blends

br, cr, dr, fr, gr, pr, tr

Consonant blends are two or more consonants that appear before or after a vowel. With *r* blends, the consonant sounds blend quickly, but they retain their sounds. For example, there are four sounds in the word *frog*: /f/ /r/ /ŏ/ /g/. But the *f* and *r* are read quickly to make a smooth sound. This week, students will learn about seven common *r* blends.

Introduction

Directions: Look at the words below. Each word has an *r* blend. Run your finger under the letters from left to right. Say one sound for each letter. Then, read the words normally. Talk about the meaning of each word.

Name: _____ Date: _____

Identification

Directions: Read the words in the Word Bank. Underline the letters that make the *r* blend in each word. Write the words next to the matching pictures.

R Blends

Word Bank

brick   crop   drink   frog   grass   truck

1.  _____

4. _____

2.  _____

5. _____

3. _____

6.  _____

Try This!

Think of a word that has an *r* blend. Tap the sounds, and write the word. Then, draw a picture to match.

Word Sort

Directions: Read the words in the Word Bank. Sort the words by consonant blends. Write them in the chart.

Word Bank

track	stuck	swing	cloth
brick	fresh	glam	plank
swam	sniff	stem	blink
club	grip	cross	trick

S Blends	
L Blends	
R Blends	

Try This!

Write each word from the Word Bank on a note card. Place the note cards around the room. Ask a friend to find the words. Read the words, and sort them a different way.

Name: _____   Date: _____

Word Play

Directions: Use the letters to make words with *r* blends. Then, choose three words, and use them in sentences. Be sure each sentence begins with a capital letter and ends with a punctuation mark.

r	f	b	c	g	i
a	k	p	m	n	l

R Blends

Words

1. _____   5. _____

2. _____   6. _____

3. _____   7. _____

4. _____   8. _____

Sentences

1. _____

2. _____

3. _____

Reading

Directions: Read the paragraph. Highlight or circle words that have *r* blends. There are six different words. Draw a picture to go with the paragraph.

All About Frogs

Frogs are interesting animals. Some can be big, and others are small. They live in different places, but most live where it is warm. They like to swim in water, and they can jump in the grass. They have long legs to help them jump. They can grip onto twigs and sticks as they jump all around. A frog will use its long tongue to catch fresh bugs as a snack. Yuck! Some people like to catch frogs and make traps to grab them. Remember to put them back in the grass or water. The frogs will thank you!

R Blends

Name: _____ Date: _____

Writing

Directions: Write the words from the Word Bank in alphabetical order. Then, choose three words, and write them in sentences. Be sure each sentence begins with a capital letter and ends with a punctuation mark.

Word Bank

brunch	bring	crash
truth	grill	trick

R Blends

Words

1. _____

2. _____

3. _____

4. _____

5. _____

6. _____

Sentences

1. _____

2. _____

3. _____

Overview

Three-Letter Blends

scr, spl, spr, str

Three-letter blends have three consonants with no vowels separating them. Just like with two-letter blends, each letter retains its sound. For example, in the word *scrap*, *s* makes the /s/ sound, *c* makes the /k/ sound, and *r* makes the /r/ sound. When read, these consonants blend quickly so that the word is read fluently as *scrap*.

Consonant Digraph Blends

thr, shr

A consonant digraph blend occurs when a digraph such as *sh* or *th* blends with another consonant, such as *r*. In contrast to three-letter blends, the digraph makes a new sound that blends with the additional consonant. For example, in the word *shrink*, the *sh* makes the sound /sh/. The individual /s/ and /h/ sounds are no longer heard.

Introduction

Directions: Place counters or coins on the dots. Listen closely as each word is read aloud slowly. Slide the counters into the boxes as you hear sounds in each word. Then, write the letters that stand for each sound in the boxes.

splash

● ● ● ● ●

throb

● ● ● ●

Name: _____   Date: _____

Identification

Directions: Read the words aloud. Draw sound boxes around each word.

Example: shrink

sh	r	i	nk

1. s h r e d

2. s p l i t

3. s c r a p

4. s p l a s h

5. s h r a n k

6. t h r a s h

7. s p r i n t

8. s t r u m

9. s c r u b

10. t h r i l l

Three-Letter Blends and Consonant Digraph Blends

Try This!

Write the words on note cards. Underline the letters that make the blends. Sort the cards by three-letter blends and consonant digraph blends.

Word Sort

Directions: Read the words in the Word Bank. Sort the words by consonant blends. Write them in the chart.

Word Bank

thrill	strum	stress	scrub
scratch	splash	sprint	scrap
strung	shrub	sprang	throb
shrank	shrill	shred	

Three-Letter Blends	
Consonant Digraph Blends	

Try This!

Search a book. Find one word with a three-letter blend and one with a consonant digraph blend. List them here.

_____ _____

Name: _____   Date: _____

Word Play

Directions: Read each clue. Complete the crossword puzzle.

Down

1. a sound made by water
4. to make smaller
5. the season after winter
6. a thread
7. to cut into tiny pieces

Across

2. to run quickly
3. to itch
4. a small plant like a bush
6. an anxious feeling
8. to cut in half

130214—180 Days™: Phonics   © Shell Education

Reading

Directions: Read the paragraph. Highlight or circle words that have three-letter blends or consonant digraph blends. There are seven different words. Then, draw pictures to match the steps of playing a guitar.

How to Play the Guitar

A guitar is a fun instrument to play. It can be hard at first, but do not stress! You will see that it is a lot of fun when you try your best and practice. First, grab your guitar and put the strap around your shoulder. The strap will keep the guitar in place. Then, press your fingers on the strings and strum the guitar. Make sure that the sound is just right. Your fingers may throb, but with practice, they will get strong. When you are ready, play for your friends and family!

Step 1	
Step 2	
Step 3	

Three-Letter Blends and Consonant Digraph Blends

Writing

Directions: Read the words in the Word Bank. Choose five words, and write them in sentences. Be sure each sentence begins with a capital letter and ends with a punctuation mark.

Word Bank

scrap	shrank	split	string	thrill
scruff	shred	sprint	struck	throb

1. _____

2. _____

3. _____

4. _____

5. _____

Try This!

Choose five words. Read each word to a friend. Have your friend tap out the sounds in the words. Then, switch roles.

Overview

Final Consonant Blends

–ft, –st, –lp, –nt, –nd, –mp

A final consonant blend is when two or more consonants are blended at the end of a word. Similar to initial consonant blends, each letter retains its sound. For example, when reading the word *soft*, you hear four sounds /s/ /ŏ/ /f/ /t/. The sounds are read together quickly to allow for fluent reading of the word. This week, students will learn about six final consonant blends.

Introduction

Directions: Look at the words below. The last two letters in each word are a final consonant blend. Run your finger under the letters from left to right. Say one sound for each letter. Then, read the words normally. Talk about the meaning of each word.

Name: _____ Date: _____

Identification

Directions: Read the words. Circle the final consonant blends (*–ft*, *–st*, *–lp*, *–nt*, *–nd*, and *–mp*).

Final Consonant Blends

ant	blend	**bond**	cast	**chant**
chest	clamp	clump	drift	help
kelp	**left**	lift	**lump**	map
pest	plump	rant	**read**	**rent**
rest	shift	sift	**skate**	spend
spent	stool	**vast**	vest	**yelp**

Try This!

Search a book. List at least five other words you can find with final consonant blends.

_____

_____

Word Sort

Directions: Read each word in the Word Bank. Sort the words by final consonant blend. Write them in the chart.

Word Bank

blend	help	mint	sand	west
camp	lamp	must	shift	yelp
gift	last	pond	spent	
gulp	left	ramp	tent	

–ft	
–st	
–lp	
–nt	
–nd	
–mp	

Final Consonant Blends

Name: _____ Date: _____

Word Play

Directions: Write the final consonant blend at the end of each set of letters. Read the words you made. The first one has been done for you.

–ft	–st	–lp
gi __ft__	fa _____	ke _____
ra _____	we _____	he _____
so _____	la _____	ye _____
li _____	be _____	pu _____

–nt	–nd	–mp
le _____	la _____	lu _____
re _____	ba _____	da _____
te _____	sa _____	ca _____
li _____	be _____	pu _____

Try This!

Look around the room. Find two other things that have final consonant blends in their names. Write the names of the objects.

_____ _____

Reading

Directions: Read each sentence. Circle the final consonant blend (*–ft*, *–st*, *–lp*, *–nt*, *–nd*, or *–mp*) in each sentence. Write the word with the blend.

1. Grandpa sent me a hat for my birthday. _____

2. Can you please help me with this box? _____

3. The wind blew leaves off the tree. _____

4. Twist the cap to take the lid off the water bottle. _____

5. Joshua loves to camp at the lake. _____

6. Please help me clean the yard. _____

7. Sasha rode her bike by the pond. _____

8. Mom wrote a list of food to buy at the store. _____

9. I lent money to my brother. _____

10. Turn the lamp off when you are done. _____

11. The loft had a bed and couch. _____

12. The dog let out a yelp when it rained. _____

Final Consonant Blends

Name: _____   Date: _____

Writing

Directions: Write the words from the Word Bank in alphabetical order. Then, choose three words, and write them in sentences. Be sure each sentence begins with a capital letter and ends with a punctuation mark.

Word Bank

blend	cast	spent
left	kelp	clump

Alphabetical Order

1. _____

2. _____

3. _____

4. _____

5. _____

6. _____

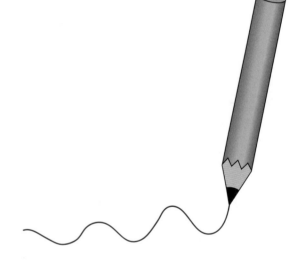

Sentences

1. _____

2. _____

3. _____

Overview

Closed-Syllable Exceptions
all, ind, ild, old, ost, olt, ull

Dividing words into chunks, or syllables, helps speed the process of decoding written text. Knowing the rules for how to divide syllables can help students read more accurately and fluently.

Closed syllables have a single vowel followed by one or more consonants, such as in *tug*, *spot*, and *twist*. A typical closed syllable has a short vowel sound. However, there are exceptions to this rule. One closed-syllable exception is when the vowel sound is long despite the word ending in one or more consonants, such as in *kind*. Other closed-syllable exceptions are the letter combinations *all* and *ull*. These letter combinations do not make the vowel sound short or long. For example, take the words *ball* and *pull*. Notice the vowels *a* and *u* do not make a short or long sound. Practice saying these sounds, and notice the differences.

Introduction

Directions: The words below are closed-syllable exceptions. This means they end with consonants but their vowels are long. Underline the final consonants in the words. Run your finger under the letters from left to right. Say one sound for each letter. Then, read the words normally.

blind   scold   most   bolt   child

Name: _____ Date: _____

Identification

Directions: Read the words. Circle the letters that make a closed-syllable exception.

Closed-Syllable Exceptions

kind   wild   cold   post   **jolt**

bolt   told   **child**   mind   stall

ball   **blind**   **molt**   **old**   host

grind   mild   **fold**   **gold**   most

sold   wind   **colt**   rind   scold

Try This!

Highlight or circle a word above that you do not know. Look it up in a dictionary or online. Write the definition, and draw a picture.

_____

_____

_____

Word Sort

Directions: Read the words in the Word Bank. Sort the words into the chart.

Word Bank

blind	cold	gift	post	swim	which
bolt	deck	grind	pull	thin	wrath
child	fall	knob	stop	thumb	

Closed-Syllable Exceptions	
Closed Syllables	

Closed-Syllable Exceptions

Name: _____   Date: _____

Word Play

Directions: Read the words in the Word Bank. Highlight or circle the words in the word search.

I	J	J	E	T	E	T	M	G	W
S	T	A	L	L	K	V	N	O	I
K	J	L	N	N	I	B	G	L	L
C	J	A	S	C	O	L	D	D	D
F	H	V	L	F	I	N	D	C	J
O	Z	G	U	O	M	O	S	T	L
Y	F	N	R	P	U	L	L	N	L
T	P	X	Q	I	M	I	L	D	Y
X	T	M	O	A	N	B	O	L	T
O	P	D	D	I	G	D	L	Q	F

Word Bank

bolt	gold	mild	pull	stall
find	grind	most	scold	wild

Reading

Directions: Read the story. Circle words with closed-syllable exceptions. Look for these patterns: *all*, *ind*, *ild*, *old*, *ost*, *olt*, and *ull*. There are six different words.

The Pot of Gold

"Happy St. Patrick's Day!" says my brother, Brad, as he jumps on my bed.

"Is it morning already?" I say as I squint at my little brother's happy face.

"Yes! Come look!" He runs down the hall, grabs a letter, and hands it to me.

This is wild! I think to myself. "What do you think, Brad? Where could it be?" I ask.

Brad looks in his backpack, and I look under the bed. He looks in the kitchen, and I look in the bathtub. We could not find the pot of gold anywhere.

> You are in luck, child!
> You have been good, I see,
> This gift is for you,
> What, and where, will it be?
>
> On this St. Patrick's Day,
> a pot of gold is what
>   you will find,
> You need to hunt for it,
> Think, use your mind!

Just then, I look outside and see the street is wet from the rain this morning. *There is always a rainbow after a storm!*

Brad and I rush out the front door and look up at the sky. Colors fly across the sky, and I smile.

"Let's go!"

Closed-Syllable Exceptions

Name: _____ Date: _____

Writing

Directions: Use the words in the Word Bank to complete the sentences.

Word Bank

ball	cold	full	grind	pull
bolt	find	gold	most	sold

1. There is a pot of _____ at the end of the rainbow.

2. The house next door was _____ to my best friend's family.

3. On a hot day, I like a _____ drink.

4. I like to read, but math is what I like the _____.

5. My mom will help me _____ my socks and shoes.

6. Did you see that _____ go across the sky?

7. I had a lot of cookies. I am _____!

8. Can you _____ the coffee this morning?

9. Please pass the _____ to the other players.

10. Darien will _____ the wagon around town.

Try This!

Choose four words from the Word Bank. Write two sentences using two of the words in each sentence.

Closed-Syllable Exceptions

Overview

Long Vowels with Silent *E*

When a consonant and the letter *e* follow a vowel, the vowel usually makes a long sound. The vowel "says its name," and the *e* at the end of the word is silent. While a breve (ŏ) is used to mark a short vowel, a macron (ō) is used to mark a long vowel. This week, students will explore long vowels with silent *es*.

Introduction

Directions: Read the words on the left. They each have a short vowel sound. Read the words on the right. The *e* at the end makes the vowels have a long sound. Write a short vowel symbol above the vowels on the left. Write a long vowel symbol above the vowels on the right. The first one has been done for you.

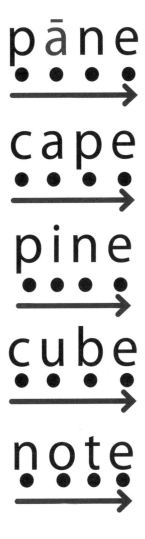

Name: _____   Date: _____

Identification

Directions: Circle the long vowel and the silent *e* in each word.

cape   safe   wave   chase   whale

dime   size   life   vine   hive

lace   mice   place   spice   trace

cage   huge   stage   page   age

hose   phone   note   close   smoke

Try This!

Put your arm out straight in front of you. Starting at your shoulder, tap down your arm for the sounds you hear in the words above. Slide your hand down your arm to say the words.

Word Sort

Directions: Read the words in the Word Bank. Sort the words by vowel sounds. Write them in the chart.

Word Bank

brake	crate	shape	space	swam
cape	price	shock	stress	time
clamp	rope	shrub	stripe	twig
crash	scratch	smoke	stuck	when

Short Vowels	
Long Vowels	

Try This!

Practice writing long-vowel words in sand, shaving cream, or rice. Say the sounds as you write the words.

Long Vowels with Silent E

Name: _____   Date: _____

Word Play

Directions: Read each word chain. Highlight or circle the letters that change.

Long Vowels with Silent *E*

shine → pine → pipe → stripe → stride

ape → grape → grade → wade → wave

hole → hope → rope → robe → globe

place → space → spice → rice → race

age → cage → stage → stake → stoke

Try This!

Make a word chain. Start with the word *cape*. Change one sound at a time. Write your new words.

cape _____ _____ _____ _____

Reading

Directions: Read the story. Circle the silent *e* words. There are 16 different words.

Kate's Big Day

It was the first day of school in the ocean, and Kate was afraid.

"What if no one likes me? I am a big blue whale, and the others are small fish. I will not fit in!" Kate cried to her mom.

"You will do great. The other students will love you!" Kate's mom said.

Kate was not so sure. She was not the same as the other students. What if they were not kind? What if she did not make any friends? The thought of being different from the other students made her nervous.

Kate and her mom swam through the waves toward low-tide waters, where she would go to school. As they got close, Kate felt tears run down her fins. It was going to be a long, hard day.

"Hi! My name is Dave! What is yours? Are you here for school?" A kind voice came from behind Kate. The dolphin swam up and smiled warmly at Kate.

"My name is Kate. Yes, I am," Kate said.

"Come over to this rock. This is where we go for attendance," Dave said.

"You go to school here, too? But you are a dolphin!"

"Why, school is for all the animals in the ocean! Some of us are huge, some of us are small. We are all different, and we are all here to learn. You will see!" Dave's face was calm and kind. It made Kate not so scared.

"I love you! Have a great day!" Mom gave a wave, and she was gone.

Kate suddenly felt excited. It *was* going to be a great day!

Long Vowels with Silent E

Name: _____ Date: _____

Writing

Directions: Write four sentences with words that have silent *E*s. Be sure each sentence begins with a capital letter and ends with a punctuation mark.

1. _____

2. _____

3. _____

4. _____

Try This!

Read your sentences to a friend. Have your friend read their sentences to you. Write the sentences your friend reads to you.

1. _____

2. _____

3. _____

4. _____

Overview

Y as Long I and Long E

The letter *y* often acts as a vowel. It can make either a long *i* or a long *e* sound. When the letter *y* is at the end of a one-syllable word, it typically makes a long *i* sound, such as in *by* or *try*. In a two-syllable word, the *y* at the end makes a long *e* sound, such as in *baby* or *cozy*. This week, students will learn about these *y* patterns.

Introduction

Directions: Read the words below. Clap the syllables in each word. Circle the words that have one syllable. Underline the words that have two syllables. Notice that the one-syllable words make the long *i* sound. The two-syllable words make the long *e* sound.

my   lazy   tiny   dry

Name: _____   Date: _____

Identification

Directions: Circle the *y* in each word. Decide whether it makes an *i* or *e* sound. Read the words aloud.

fly	why	lacy	crazy	**shy**
spicy	my	**lady**	cry	pricy
cozy	by	**lazy**	style	type
dry	tiny	**shiny**	**navy**	sky

Try This!

Write a short poem using some of the words above.

_____

_____

_____

Word Sort

Directions: Read the words in the Word Bank. Sort the words by the sound the *y* makes. Write them in the chart.

Word Bank

by	cry	happy	shiny	spicy
candy	fly	lady	shy	taffy
cozy	fry	my	sky	try
crazy	funny	navy	sly	why

Y as Long I	
Y as Long E	

Y as Long I and Long E

Name: _____ Date: _____

Word Play

Directions: Read the words in the Word Bank. Highlight or circle the words in the word search.

Y as Long *I* and Long *E*

```
Q   S   T   G   N   Q   I   T   E   B

Y   K   Q   C   R   A   Z   Y   J   Y

R   Y   B   C   W   H   Y   J   W   N

T   L   A   Z   Y   S   F   N   O   A

J   K   S   Y   M   F   H   B   Z   V

G   P   N   H   Y   W   S   Y   Q   Y

O   U   R   B   I   P   A   F   V   U

J   W   S   I   H   N   O   E   F   U

L   A   T   E   C   J   Y   S   X   P

O   Y   Y   R   S   Y   Q   I   H   E
```

Word Bank

by	lazy	navy	shiny	sky
crazy	my	pricy	shy	why

Name: _____ Date: _____

Reading

Directions: Circle the words that have a *y* as a long vowel. Some sentences have more than one. Write these words.

1. The baby will cry for her mom. _____

2. The shiny ring is safe in the box. _____

3. José and Judy have a big baseball game today. _____

4. Why is the wind so cold? _____

5. I hope my sister will share her candy with me. _____

6. When it is rainy, I am lazy. _____

7. Kendrick is a funny friend. _____

8. The saltwater taffy is a gift from her trip. _____

9. The lady has five cats. _____

10. How do you make the dish less spicy? _____

Try This!

Think of a word ending with *y*. Tap the sounds, and write the word. Then, draw a picture to match.

_____

Y as Long *I* and Long *E*

Name: _____   Date: _____

Writing

Directions: Write the words from the Word Bank in alphabetical order. Then, choose three words, and write them in sentences. Be sure each sentence begins with a capital letter and ends with a punctuation mark.

Word Bank

shiny	tiny	lady
fly	shy	type

Alphabetical Order

1. _____

2. _____

3. _____

4. _____

5. _____

6. _____

Sentences

1. _____

2. _____

3. _____

Overview

Vowel Teams *ee* and *ea*

When two vowels are presented together, they usually make one long vowel sound. This is called a *vowel team*. The first vowel in the pair is usually the vowel that "says its name." For example, the letters *ea* represent /ē/ in the word *read*. There are three sounds in the word *read*: /r/ /ē/ /d/. The *ee* and *ea* vowel teams are usually positioned in the middle of a word or syllable, but they can also be at the beginning or end.

Introduction

Directions: Place counters or coins on the dots. Listen closely as each word is read aloud slowly. Slide the counters into the boxes as you hear sounds in each word. Write the letters that stand for each sound in the boxes.

seed

treat

Name: _____   Date: _____

Identification

Directions: Read the words aloud. Draw sound boxes around each word.

Example: speech

s	p	ee	ch

Vowel Teams *ee, ea*

1. q u e e n

2. b e a c h

3. c h e e s e

4. t e a c h

5. w h e a t

6. d r e a m

7. s l e e p

8. t e e t h

9. c h e e r

10. p e a c h

Try This!

Write the words above on craft sticks. Write "Oh, no!" on a few more craft sticks. Put all the craft sticks into a cup. Take turns with a friend picking a craft stick and reading the word. If you choose an "Oh, no!" stick, return all your words to the cup.

Word Sort

Directions: Read the words in the Word Bank. Sort the words by vowel team spelling. Write them in the chart.

Word Bank

bead	deep	leave	speak
cheap	feet	meat	sweet
cheer	geese	queen	teeth
clean	green	reach	tree

ee	
ea	

Try This!

Write each word from the Word Bank on a note card. Place the note cards around the room. Ask a friend to find the words. Read the words, and sort them a different way.

Name: _____   Date: _____

Word Play

Directions: Use the letters to make words with vowel teams *ee* or *ea*. Then, choose three words, and use them in sentences. Be sure each sentence begins with a capital letter and ends with a punctuation mark.

e	a	s	c	h	p
l	t	b	f	n	r

Vowel Teams ee, ea

Words

1. _____   5. _____

2. _____   6. _____

3. _____   7. _____

4. _____   8. _____

Sentences

1. _____

2. _____

3. _____

Try This!

Look at the words you made. Use clay to roll four small balls. Squish a ball for each sound you hear in the words. Write the number of sounds next to each word above.

Reading

Directions: Read the passage. Highlight or circle the *ee* and *ea* vowel teams. There are 14 different words.

The Beach Trip

Every summer, Lilly and her family go to the beach. Her favorite thing to do is sit by the water and feel the waves crash at her feet. She loves to feel the wind brush against her cheek. This year, Lilly wants to bring her best friend, Kyra.

"Please! Please!" Lilly cries to her mom. "We do not get to see each other very much. We do not go to the same school. The trip will be so much more fun with a friend to play with." Lilly thinks of swimming in the sea and playing in the sand with her best friend.

"I will ask Kyra's gram if she can come. Now, go pack. We will be there for a whole week! You need to get your things!" Mom says.

Lilly's face lights up with a big grin. She runs to her bedroom to pack. She puts her brush, seven tops, and seven pants in her bag. She makes sure to grab all the things she needs. She runs down the steps to see if Kyra can come.

Beep! Beep! The phone on the table makes Lilly freeze. *Will Kyra be able to come?* she thinks.

"Kyra will come with us!" Mom says. "She is on her way home from cheer camp, and she will pack. We will pick her up on the way. Now, let's go! Put all your things in the back of the car!"

Lilly jumps up and down. Her friend will come! She cannot wait until they reach the sea. It will be the best trip yet!

Vowel Teams ee, ea

Name: _____   Date: _____

Writing

Directions: Read the words in the Word Bank. Choose five words, and write them in sentences. Be sure each sentence begins with a capital letter and ends with a punctuation mark.

Word Bank

clean	freeze	read	sleet	steep
east	queen	screech	squeeze	teach

1. _____

2. _____

3. _____

4. _____

5. _____

Vowel Teams *ee, ea*

Overview

Vowel Teams *ai* and *ay*

Similar to *ee* and *ea*, the letters *ai* and *ay* form vowel teams. When *ai* or *ay* are presented together, they usually make the long *a* sound. For example, in the word *rain*, there are three sounds—/r/ /ā/ /n/. The letters *ai* work together to make the /ā/ sound. The *ai* vowel team is usually positioned in the middle of a word or syllable, while the *ay* vowel team is usually positioned at the end of a word or syllable.

Introduction

Directions: Look at your face in a mirror. Make the short *a* sound. Notice the shape your mouth makes. Then, make the long *a* sound. Talk about the different shapes your mouth makes with these sounds.

130214—180 Days™: Phonics

Name: _____   Date: _____

Identification

Directions: Read the words in the Word Bank. Underline the letters that make the vowel team in each word. Write the words next to the matching pictures.

Word Bank

clay	hay	paint	pay	snail	train

1.  _____

2.  _____

3. _____

4.  _____

5.  _____

6.  _____

Try This!

Search a book. Find five other words that have *ai* or *ay* vowel teams. Write the words.

_____ _____ _____ _____ _____

Word Sort

Directions: Read the words in the Word Bank. Sort the words by vowel team spelling. Write them in the chart.

Word Bank

clay	gray	rainy	sway
drain	hail	raise	tray
frail	hay	snail	waist
grain	play	stray	way

ai	
ay	

Try This!

Skywrite the words from the Word Bank. Say the sounds as you skywrite.

Name: _____   Date: _____

Word Play

Directions: Choose four words from the previous page. Write them on the lines. Read the words aloud. Slide counters or coins into the boxes as you say the sounds in the words.

1. _____

Try This!

Practice writing the words in sand, shaving cream, or rice. Say the sounds as you write the words.

2. _____

_____

_____

3. _____

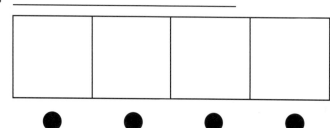

_____

_____

4. _____

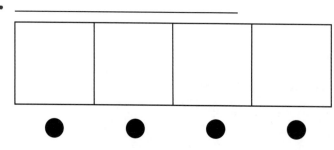

Vowel Teams *ai, ay*

Reading

Directions: Read the poem. Circle the words with *ai* and *ay* vowel teams. There are five different words. Underline the rhyming words.

Vowel Teams *ai, ay*

Rainy Day Blues

The rain falls on my porch
Drip, drop, drip, drop, all day
The sun will not peek through, it seems
I hope it will come out to stay

The rain falls on my window
I peer out while I sit, and I wait
Maybe the rain will stop falling soon
I think that would be just great!

Name: _____ Date: _____

Writing

Directions: Write four sentences with words that have *ai* or *ay* vowel teams. Be sure each sentence begins with a capital letter and ends with a punctuation mark.

1. _____

2. _____

3. _____

4. _____

Try This!

Read your sentences to a friend. Have your friend read their sentences to you. Write the sentences your friend reads to you.

1. _____

2. _____

3. _____

4. _____

Vowel Teams *ai, ay*

Overview

Vowel Teams *oa, ow,* and *oe*

Similar to *ee, ea, ai,* and *ay,* the letters *oa, ow,* and *oe* form vowel teams. When *oa, ow,* or *oe* are presented together, they usually make the long *o* sound. For example, in the word *boat,* there are three sounds: /b/ /ō/ /t/. The letters *oa* work together to make the /ō/ sound. The *oa* vowel team is usually positioned in the middle of a word or syllable. The *ow* and *oe* vowel teams are usually positioned at the end of a word or syllable. The *ow* vowel team is positioned in the middle of a word when it is followed by an *n* or *l*.

Introduction

Directions: Look at the words below. Circle the vowel team in each word. These vowel teams all say the long *o* sound.

boat   grow   toe

An easy way to remember the sounds of vowel teams is the chant "When two vowels go walking, the first one does the talking!"

Name: _____   Date: _____

Identification

Directions: Look at the pictures. Write the missing vowel teams to complete the words.

 s _____ p

 r _____ d

  m _____

 sn _____

  pill _____

  yell_____

 t _____

 f _____

 c _____ t

Try This!

Put your arm out straight in front of you. Starting at your shoulder, tap down your arm for the sounds you hear in the words above. Slide your hand down your arm to say the words.

Word Sort

Directions: Read the words in the Word Bank. Sort the words by vowel team spelling. Write them in the chart.

Word Bank

coach	grow	road	toast
coast	Joe	show	toe
doe	know	soap	window
float	pillow	throat	woe

oa	
ow	
oe	

Try This!

Search a book. List at least five other words you can find with a long *o* vowel team.

_____ _____ _____ _____ _____

Vowel Teams *oa, ow, oe*

Word Play

Directions: Read each word chain. Highlight or circle the letters that change.

coat → goat → float → flat → flap

low → glow → grow → throw → row

toe → woe → wall → ball → stall

soak → soap → sap → clap → clam

load → road → rod → rode → ride

Try This!

Make a word chain. Start with the word *coach*. Change one sound at a time. Write your new words.

coach _____ _____ _____ _____

Name: _____ Date: _____

Reading

Directions: Read the passage. Circle the words with *oa*, *ow*, and *oe* vowel teams. There are seven different words.

Joan's Snow Day

Beep! Beep! I groan as I reach my weak, sleepy arm out to stop the dreadful sound. I rub my eyes and force them open to peek at the time on the clock. *6:30 a.m.* A chill dances through me, and I pull my sheet above my head. *It is so cold! I cannot get out of bed!* I think to myself as I shut my eyes once more. The test I have later today flashes in my mind, and a wave of stress flows through me.

"Joan! Come look out the window!" yells Mom from the kitchen down the hall.

I slowly make my way to the kitchen window. As I peer outside, I see tiny flakes of snow sway in the wind, and a white sheet covers the grass I had just played in the day before. Mom's phone shakes on the kitchen table as the words *NO SCHOOL* light up across the screen. Calm vibes rush from my head to my toes, and a smile creeps across my face. As I imagine a cozy day inside, I feel a little warmer already.

Vowel Teams *oa, ow, oe*

Name: _____ Date: _____

Writing

Directions: Use the words in the Word Bank to complete the sentences.

Word Bank

coat	goat	oak	shadow	throw
follow	know	road	slowly	toe

1. In the winter, the _____ rack is full.

2. When you clean, _____ out your trash.

3. I hit my _____ on the bench. Ouch!

4. I _____ how to write funny stories.

5. The _____ needs a bath and then a brush.

6. My _____ follows me wherever I go!

7. The _____ is very rocky and bumpy.

8. Can you drive the car _____?

9. Please _____ me to the bookstore.

10. I like to play in the _____ tree at my house.

Try This!

Write a short story using some of the words in the Word Bank. Read your story to a friend.

Overview

Vowel Teams *igh* and *ie*

When two or more vowels are presented together, they usually make one long vowel sound. The first vowel in the team is usually the vowel that "says its name." For example, the letters *ie* represent /ī/ in the word *pie*. There are two sounds in the word *pie*: /p/ /ī/. The *ie* vowel team is usually positioned at the end of a short word. The *igh* vowel team is generally positioned in the middle or end of a word or syllable.

Introduction

Directions: Look at the words below. Circle the *ie* or *igh* vowel team in each word. These vowel teams all make the long *i* sound.

light   pie   lie

high   thigh   tie

Name: _____   Date: _____

Identification

Directions: Read the words. Circle the words that have *igh* and *ie* vowel teams.

blow   breeze   bright   cheese   **coat**

daisy   fight   **flight**   glow   high

know   **lie**   **might**   **night**   paint

peace   pie   **please**   **queen**   right

sheep   soap   speak   stay   **team**

thigh   throw   **tie**   tray   waist

Try This!

Skywrite the letters *igh* and *ie*. Say the sounds as
you skywrite. Then, skywrite five of the words above.

Word Sort

Directions: Read the words in the Word Bank. Sort the words by vowel team spelling. Write them in the chart.

Word Bank

bright	high	night	slight
die	knight	pie	thigh
flight	lie	sigh	tie
fright	might	sight	tight

igh	
ie	

Try This!

Write the words in the Word Bank on note cards. Sort the words differently. Get creative!

Name: _____ Date: _____

Word Play

Directions: Read each clue. Complete the crossword puzzle. Each word has the *igh* or *ie* vowel team.

Down

1. the opposite of loose
3. the opposite of dark
4. a time when something flies
6. a dessert, usually served on Thanksgiving

Across

2. to make a knot
3. the opposite of wrong
4. an argument
5. to not tell the truth
7. when there is a lot of light
8. the opposite of day

Reading

Directions: Read the poem. Circle words that have the *igh* and *ie* vowel teams. There are five different words. Highlight the rhyming words.

The Night Sky

The stars way up high,
are little specks in the night sky.
They shine, and they gleam,
They are so much more than they seem!

The moon, with its glow,
How far away? I do not know.
Its round face sends us a smile,
for just a short little while.

Just then, a star takes flight,
sent away, out of sight.
Look quick, watch it go!
Maybe more will follow.

And on this clear, brisk night,
I look up with delight.
For soon, the sun will come to play,
As night turns back to day.

Vowel Teams *igh, ie*

Name: _____ Date: _____

Writing

Directions: Write four sentences with words that have *igh* or *ie* vowel teams. Be sure each sentence begins with a capital letter and ends with a punctuation mark.

1. _____

2. _____

3. _____

4. _____

Try This!

Read your sentences to a friend. Have your friend read their sentences to you. Write the sentences your friend reads to you.

1. _____

2. _____

3. _____

4. _____

Vowel Teams *igh, ie*

Overview

Vowel Teams *ew*, *ue*, and *oo*

Vowel teams *ew* and *ue* each have two sounds. They can both have the long *u* sound (*few* and *hue*) and the /oo/ sound (*threw* and *blue*). These spellings are usually positioned at the ends of words or syllables.

The vowel team *oo* is usually pronounced as either a long sound, such as in *moon*, or a short sound, such as in *book*.

Introduction

Directions: Place counters or coins on the dots. Listen closely as each word is read aloud slowly. Slide the counters into the boxes as you hear the sounds in each word. Talk about the different sounds you hear. Then, write the letters that stand for each sound in the boxes.

glue

threw

hook

boot

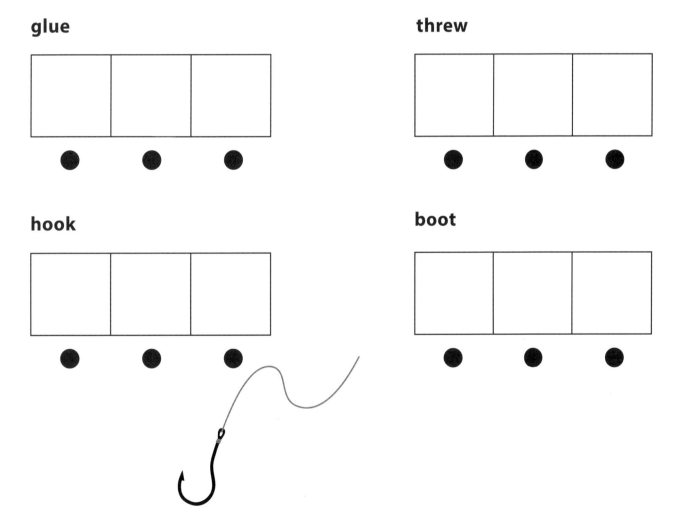

Name: _____ Date: _____

Identification

Directions: Highlight or circle the *ue*, *ew*, and *oo* vowel teams in the words. Then, read the words aloud.

hue	clue	glue	**blue**	**true**
spook	**booth**	hoop	**mood**	bloom
foot	**wood**	good	hook	shook
knew	stew	**grew**	**threw**	drew
look	**gloom**	**blew**	flew	**dew**

Try This!

Place the counters on the dots. Choose five words from above. Slide the counters into the boxes as you say the sounds in the words.

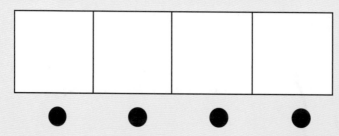

Word Sort

Directions: Read the words in the Word Bank. Sort the words by vowel team spelling. Write them in the chart.

Word Bank

blew	broom	hood	stew
bloom	cook	screw	threw
blue	droop	shook	troop
book	glue	spook	zoom

ue	
ew	
/oo/ as in book	
/oo/ as in moon	

Try This!

Search the room for more words with these vowel teams. Write three words in the chart.

Vowel Teams *ew, ue, oo*

Name: _____   Date: _____

Word Play

Directions: Read the words. Change the sounds to make new words. Then, choose three words, and use them in sentences.

1. blew ➝ ☐ lew   6. food ➝ ☐ ood

2. threw ➝ ☐ rew   7. book ➝ ☐ ook

3. blue ➝ ☐ lue   8. good ➝ ☐ ood

4. hue ➝ ☐ ue   9. wood ➝ woo ☐

5. bloom ➝ ☐ loom   10. hoop ➝ ☐ oop

Sentences

1. _____

2. _____

3. _____

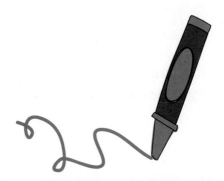

Vowel Teams ew, ue, oo

Reading

Directions: Read the paragraph. Circle words with the *ew, ue,* and *oo* vowel teams. There are five different words. Then, draw pictures to match the steps of making a book.

How to Make a Nonfiction Book

You can write your own nonfiction book—it is true! Think of a few topics you know a lot about. Maybe you know a lot about animals, your favorite food, or a place you have been to. Now that you have your topic, your first step is to make a plan. Look for facts about your topic. The facts will keep your book interesting! Then, begin your first draft of your book. Take all your facts, and put them into complete sentences. Edit your writing to be sure that your ideas are clear. Last, publish your writing! Make sure your writing is neat. Create a cover, glue the pages together, and draw a picture on the cover. Your book is ready to share!

Vowel Teams *ew, ue, oo*

Step 1	
Step 2	
Step 3	
Step 4	

Name: _____ Date: _____

Writing

Directions: Read the words in the Word Bank. Choose five words, and write them in sentences. Be sure each sentence begins with a capital letter and ends with a punctuation mark.

Word Bank

| bloom | clue | glue | moon | spoon |
| blue | flew | look | moose | threw |

1. _____

2. _____

3. _____

4. _____

5. _____

Try This!

Choose five words. Read each word to a friend. Have your friend tap the sounds in the words. Then, switch roles.

Overview

Vowel Teams *au* and *aw*

The letters *au* and *aw* are vowel teams that represent one sound, /aw/. The sound is similar to short *o*, but is formed farther back in the mouth. Notice the subtle differences in the words *hot* and *pawn*. The *au* spelling pattern is typically used in the middle of words, such as in *launch*. The *aw* spelling pattern is typically used at the end of words, except when followed by an *n* or *l*, such as in *shawl*.

Introduction

Directions: Place counters or coins on the dots. Listen closely as each word is read aloud slowly. Slide the counters into the boxes as you hear sounds in each word. Then, write the letters that stand for each sound in the boxes. Talk about how the *o* sounds different from the *au* and *aw* vowel teams.

dawn

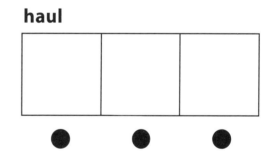

haul

fawn

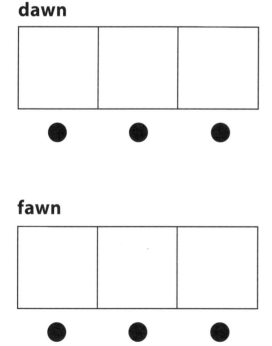

Name: _____   Date: _____

Identification

Directions: Read the words aloud. Draw sound boxes around each word.

Example: hawk

Vowel Teams au, aw

1. h a u l

2. f l a w

3. s a w

4. l a u n c h

5. s t r a w

6. f a u l t

7. c r a w l

8. v a u l t

9. y a w n

10. s h a w l

Try This!

Choose five words. Read each word to a friend. Have your friend tap out the sounds in the words and spell the words. Then, switch roles.

Word Sort

Directions: Read the words in the Word Bank. Sort the words by vowel team spelling. Write them in the chart.

Word Bank

cause	fault	pause	shawl
claw	flaw	paw	straw
crawl	hawk	sauce	vault
draw	launch	saw	yawn

au	
aw	

Try This!

Choose two words from the Word Bank. Write a sentence using both words. Share your sentence with a friend.

© Shell Education

Vowel Teams *au, aw*

Name: _____ Date: _____

Word Play

Directions: Choose four words from the previous page. Write them on the lines. Read the words aloud. Slide counters or coins into the boxes as you say the sounds in the words.

1. _____

2. _____

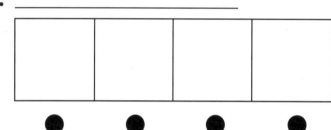

3. _____

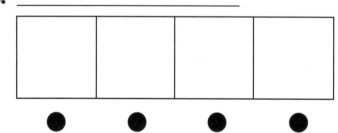

4. _____

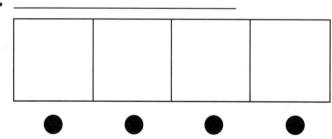

Try This!

Use letter tiles or magnets to build words with vowel teams *au* and *aw*. Write five of them.

AU
AW

_____

_____

_____

_____

_____

 130214—180 Days™: Phonics

Reading

Directions: Circle the words with *au* and *aw* vowel teams in the sentences. Write these words.

1. I watched the hawk swoop over the river. _____

2. I like to draw the beach in art class. _____

3. The crab claw is sharp. _____

4. Pause the show so I can go to the bathroom. _____

5. Do you like pizza with a lot of sauce? _____

6. She began to crawl with the baby. _____

7. Here is a straw for your drink. _____

8. It is not your fault the toy is broken. _____

9. I saw the boy score a point in the game. _____

10. What will cause the wind to blow?_____

Vowel Teams *au, aw*

Name: _____   Date: _____

Writing

Directions: Write the words from the Word Bank in alphabetical order. Then, choose three words, and write them in sentences. Be sure each sentence begins with a capital letter and ends with a punctuation mark.

Word Bank

lawn	straw	hawk
fault	launch	pause

Vowel Teams *au, aw*

Alphabetical Order

1. _____

2. _____

3. _____

4. _____

5. _____

6. _____

Sentences

1. _____

2. _____

3. _____

Overview

Review: Vowel Teams

When two or more vowels are presented together, they usually make one long vowel sound. The first vowel in the pair is typically the vowel that "says its name." There are a few vowel teams that follow different patterns. The *oo* vowel team has two sounds, such as in *book* and *moon*. The *au* and *aw* vowel teams both represent the /aw/ sound.

Introduction

Directions: Look at the words below. Run your finger under the letters from left to right. Say one sound for each letter or vowel team. Then, read the words normally. Talk about the different vowel teams.

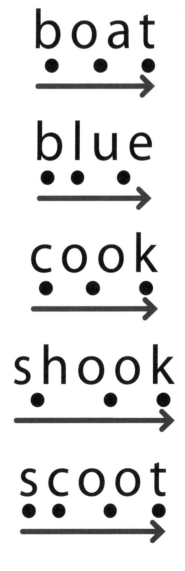

Name: _____ Date: _____

Identification

Directions: Look at the pictures. Write the missing vowel teams to complete the words.

 b _____ ch

 b _____ k

 n _____ t

 sn _____

 dr _____

 gl _____

 sn _____ l

 l _____ nch

 p _____

Try This!

Fold a sheet of paper in half horizontally. Then, fold it into thirds vertically. You will have six boxes. Write six vowel teams you have learned about at the top of each box. Then, draw a picture of a word that has that vowel team.

Word Sort

Directions: Read the words in the Word Bank. Sort the words by vowel team spelling. Write them in the chart.

Word Bank

boat	goat	moon	play	train
dew	lie	mow	quail	tray
feet	low	night	reach	true
flight	meat	pie	row	week

Long A *ai/ay*	
Long E *ee/ea*	
Long I *igh/ie*	
Long O *oa/ow/oe*	
Long U *(ew/ue/oo)*	

Name: _____ Date: _____

Word Play

Directions: Read the words in the Word Bank. Highlight or circle the words in the word search.

```
Q  U  A  I  L  C  O  U  O  F
B  T  Y  F  Z  U  R  J  T  A
S  Q  H  G  M  T  I  O  U  U
C  G  F  R  R  B  H  P  W  L
O  R  S  S  E  I  D  I  N  T
O  C  E  O  H  W  T  R  G  M
P  T  R  A  I  Z  Z  H  Q  H
P  R  P  A  C  P  E  E  L  U
B  U  E  P  W  H  B  E  B  R
Y  E  P  T  D  L  Z  C  M  C
```

Word Bank

crawl	fault	quail	scoop	threw
crow	peel	reach	thigh	true

Reading

Directions: Read the story. Circle the words with vowel teams. There are 26 different words.

The Surprise

"Come on, Reed! Come outside to play!" I yell as I race into the yard.

"I will be right there!" Reed exclaims.

As I run through the yard, I feel the warm sunshine. The past few days have been cold, so I stop to take it in. In a few weeks, the snow will drape the grass, and everything will freeze.

"Let's play hide and seek! You hide!" yells Reed from the back steps.

Reed covers his eyes as he says, "One…two…three…." I race to find a hiding spot. The large tree in our yard is my favorite. I climb until I find the perfect spot.

Just then, I hear a soft sound from the next branch. I peer closely and see a little cat. Her fur is a peach color with white spots on her back. She is at peace, but then I think of the cold coming soon. What will we do with this cat?

"Reed, come look!" I say, no longer thinking about the game.

"Joe, what are we going to do?" Reed says. "This cat will freeze if we don't do something."

"Mom will know what to do," I say. "Let's go get this cat some help!"

We yell for Mom to come help us. She brings some milk and a blanket, then goes back inside to call for help.

"We saved the day! Without our help, who knows what would have happened," I say.

"We make a great team!" Reed says.

Before going back into the house, I turn and look back at the tree. The small cat climbs down and laps up the milk. I smile.

Review: Vowel Teams

Name: _____ Date: _____

Writing

Directions: Write four sentences with vowel-team words. Be sure each sentence begins with a capital letter and ends with a punctuation mark.

1. _____

2. _____

3. _____

4. _____

Try This!

Read your sentences to a friend. Have your friend read their sentences to you. Write the sentences your friend reads to you.

1. _____

2. _____

3. _____

4. _____

Overview

Diphthongs *oi* and *oy*

A diphthong, also called a *gliding vowel*, is a combination of two vowels in one syllable. The vowel sound begins as one vowel and glides to the next vowel sound, such as in *boil* and *toy*. The /oy/ sound is typically spelled *oi* in the middle of words, such as in *coil* and *spoil*. When the /oy/ sound is at the end of words, it is typically spelled *oy*, such as in *boy* and *coy*.

Introduction

Directions: The /oy/ sound starts in the back of the mouth with rounded lips. Then, it glides to the front of the mouth with a smiley shape. Practice making this sound in front of a mirror. Watch how your mouth moves.

Name: _____   Date: _____

Identification

Directions: Read the words aloud. Draw sound boxes around each word.

Example: spoil

1. j o y

2. o i n k

3. b o y

4. o i l

5. j o i n

6. b o i l

7. f o i l

8. t o y

9. s o i l

10. c o y

Diphthongs *oi, oy*

Try This!

Search a book. List three other words you can find with *oi* and *oy* diphthongs.

_____ _____ _____

Word Sort

Directions: Read the words in the Word Bank. Sort the words by /oy/ spelling. Write them in the chart.

Diphthongs *oi, oy*

Word Bank

boil	enjoy	noise	soil
boy	join	oink	soy
broil	joy	ploy	toy
coin	moist	point	voice

oi	
oy	

Try This!

Before sorting the words, write them on note cards. Place the note cards around the room. Ask a friend to find the words. Then, read the words and sort them a different way.

Name: _____ Date: _____

Word Play

Directions: Use the letters to make words with *oi* and *oy* diphthongs. Then, choose three words, and use them in sentences. Be sure each sentence begins with a capital letter and ends with a punctuation mark.

o	i	y	l	n
p	b	t	s	c

Words

1. _____   5. _____

2. _____   6. _____

3. _____   7. _____

4. _____   8. _____

Sentences

1. _____

2. _____

3. _____

130214—180 Days™: Phonics

Name: _____ Date: _____

Reading

Directions: Read the recipe. Circle the words with *oi* and *oy* diphthongs. There are four different words.

• Recipe •

Roasted Veggies

Ingredients

- 1 tbsp oil
- 1 cup broccoli
- 1 cup cauliflower
- 1 cup carrots
- Salt and pepper, to taste

Steps

1. Preheat your oven to 350 degrees Fahrenheit.

2. Put foil on a sheet pan. Put some oil on the foil to keep the veggies from sticking.

3. Spread the veggies on the sheet pan.

4. Put a bit more oil on top of the veggies. Season with salt and pepper to taste.

5. Put the pan of veggies in the oven to roast for 20 minutes.

6. Check them after 20 minutes. Broil them for 5 minutes more until they are crispy.

7. Enjoy your roasted veggies as a tasty snack or side dish!

Diphthongs *oi, oy*

Name: _____ Date: _____

Writing

Directions: Use the words in the Word Bank to complete the sentences.

Diphthongs *oi, oy*

Word Bank

boil	choices	enjoy	moist	soil
boy	coin	foil	noise	toy

1. Make sure the _____ gets watered.

2. Put _____ over the food to keep it hot.

3. My favorite _____ to play with is a doll.

4. My teacher says to make good _____ at school.

5. The _____ has short brown hair.

6. We _____ going to swim at the community pool.

7. The concert was great, but there was a lot of _____.

8. I found a gold _____ in my pencil case.

9. _____ the water to cook the vegetables.

10. The birthday cake was sweet and _____.

Try This!

Highlight or circle an unknown word. Use the internet or a dictionary to find the definition. Write the definition, and draw a picture.

Overview

Diphthongs *ou* and *ow*

A diphthong is a combination of two letters that work together to make one vowel sound. The vowel sound changes, or glides, as it is being pronounced. The sound /ow/ can be spelled two ways. When the /ow/ sound is in the middle of a word or syllable, it can be spelled *ou*, as in *house*. When the /ow/ sound is at the middle or end of a word or syllable, it can be spelled *ow*, as in *cow*.

Introduction

Directions: The /ow/ sound begins in the front of the mouth with open lips. Then, it glides to the back of the mouth with closed lips. Practice making this sound in front of a mirror. Talk about how this sound is similar to and different from how you make the /oy/ sound.

Name: _____   Date: _____

Identification

Directions: Read the words in the Word Bank. Highlight or circle the letters that make the /ow/ sound. Write the words next to the matching pictures.

Diphthongs *ou, ow*

Word Bank

| clown | count | cow | house | mouth | shout |

1. _____

2.  _____

3.  _____

4.  _____

5.  _____

6. _____

Try This!

Skywrite the letters *ou* and *ow*. Say the sounds as you skywrite. Then, skywrite the words in the Word Bank.

Word Sort

Directions: Read the words in the Word Bank. Sort the words by *ou* and *ow* spellings. Write them in the chart.

Word Bank

brow	cow	mouse	sound
cloud	crowd	plow	sour
couch	found	pouch	wow
count	loud	shout	

ou	
ow	

Try This!

Write the words in the Word Bank on note cards. Sort the words differently. Get creative!

Name: _____ Date: _____

Word Play

Directions: Choose four words from the previous page. Write them on the lines. Read the words aloud. Slide counters or coins into the boxes as you say the sounds in the words.

Diphthongs *ou, ow*

1. _____

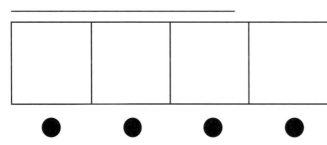

2. _____

Try This!

Make a word chain. Start with the word *found*. Change one sound at a time. Write your new words.

found

_____

_____

_____

_____

3. _____

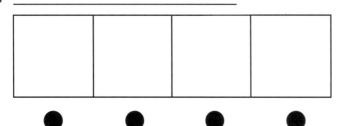

4. _____

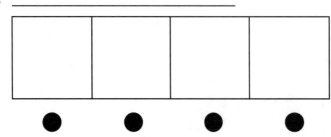

Reading

Directions: Read the poem. Circle the words with *ou* and *ow* diphthongs. There are 11 different words.

A Bug's Home

Soon, this seed will sprout.
I have no doubt!
It will grow big and grow tall.
It will be the best home of all!

The leaves will be bright and green,
Giving much more shade than they seem.
The bright pink petals will be soft.
It'll be just perfect for a cozy loft!

My bug friends will say, "Wow!"
"Where did you find that home? How?"
I will feel so happy and so proud
Of my home that's as tall as a cloud.

As I drift off into this dream,
Things are not as they seem.
For this seed that I found,
It still needs to grow in the ground.

I watch, and I wait.
This home will be just great!
But then, what's that I hear?
Is that a bark? It's coming near!

Just then, a big hound,
Digs up the soft ground.
It puts in its long snout,
And digs that seed out!

Diphthongs *ou, ow*

130214—180 Days™: Phonics   **135**

Name: _____   Date: _____

Writing

Directions: Read the words in the Word Bank. Choose five words, and write them in sentences. Be sure each sentence begins with a capital letter and ends with a punctuation mark.

Word Bank

brow	flour	our	proud	sound
cloud	how	plow	shout	spout

1. _____

2. _____

3. _____

4. _____

5. _____

Try This!

Write a short poem using some words from the Word Bank. Read it to a friend.

_____

_____

_____

Overview

R-Controlled Vowels

An *r*-controlled vowel is a vowel immediately followed by the letter *r*. The vowel is no longer pronounced as a long or short sound. Instead, the letter combination represents one sound. Often called the *bossy r*, the *r* takes over the vowel sound. Look at the word *car*. There are two sounds: /c/ /ar/. The /er/ sound is a common *r*-controlled vowel and can be spelled many ways: *ar*, *er*, *ir*, *or*, and *ur*.

Introduction

Directions: Place counters or coins on the dots. Listen closely as each word is read aloud slowly. Slide the counters into the boxes as you hear sounds in each word. Talk about the different sounds you hear. Notice that the *r* takes over the vowels. Then, write the letters that stand for each sound in the boxes.

barn

perch

thorn

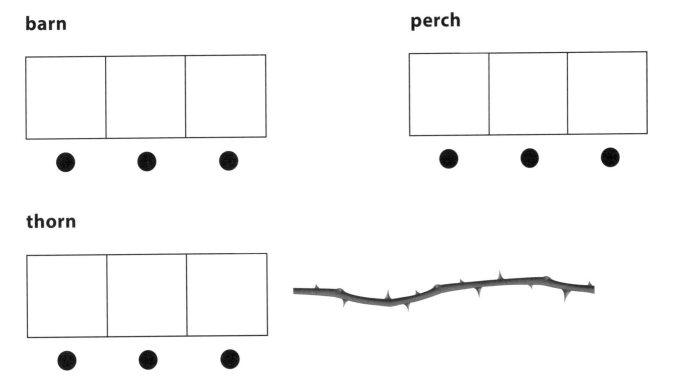

Name: _____ Date: _____

Identification

Directions: Read the words aloud. Draw sound boxes around each word.

Example: spark

s	p	ar	k

1. s h a r k

2. m a r c h

3. h u r t

4. c u r l y

5. s q u i r t

6. c h i r p

7. n o r t h

8. s t o r m

9. s c a r f

10. s p o r t

Try This!

Fold a sheet of paper in half horizontally. Then, fold it into thirds vertically. You will have six boxes. Label the first box *R-Controlled Vowels.* Label the top of each other box *ar, er, ir, or,* and *ur.* In each of these boxes, draw a picture of a word that has the labeled *r*-controlled vowel.

Word Sort

Directions: Read the words in the Word Bank. Sort the words by *r*-controlled vowels. Write them in the chart.

Word Bank

chirp	fern	north	squirt
church	girl	perch	star
curb	harp	scarf	storm
dark	march	sport	thorn

ar	
er	
ir	
or	
ur	

R-Controlled Vowels

Name: _____   Date: _____

Word Play

Directions: Read each clue. Complete the crossword puzzle. Each word has an *ar*, *er*, *ir*, *or*, or *ur* pattern.

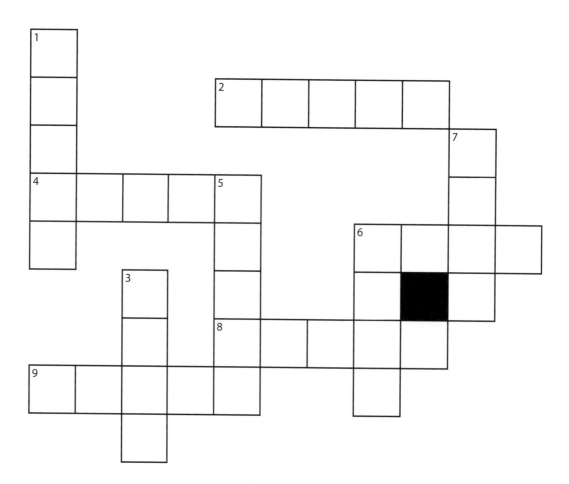

Down

1. the number that comes after 39
3. something that is not easy
5. someone who takes care of others in a hospital
6. when something gets too hot
7. an action word

Across

2. the sound that birds make
4. a sharp point on the stem of a rose
6. the sound a dog makes
8. when there is rain, lightning, and thunder
9. to come together

Reading

Directions: Read the passage. Circle words with *r*-controlled vowels. There are nine different words. Then, draw a park in your community.

The Park

A park is a great place to go. There are many different things to do there. It is a fun place to spend time with family and friends. A park is a great place to go if you do not have a yard where you live. Whether it is warm or cold outside, there is plenty to do!

Many parks have playgrounds for children to play. Girls and boys can jump, swing, and run around. Kids can bring their friends or make new ones. Playing at the playground is a fun activity for a sunny day.

There is also a lot of open space at the park. There is plenty of grass to run around in or to play a game like soccer. Some parks have soccer nets you can use to play a game. Many people also bring balls to toss or gear to practice their favorite sports.

The park is a great place to be active. People can go for a short or long run. Many people walk or play with their dogs at the park. Bringing your furry friend will make them very happy!

There are many perks to visiting the park. There is a lot to see and a lot to do. The next time there is a sunny day, visit the park!

R-Controlled Vowels

Name: _____   Date: _____

Writing

Directions: Write the words from the Word Bank in alphabetical order. Then, choose three words, and write them in sentences. Be sure each sentence begins with a capital letter and ends with a punctuation mark.

Word Bank

storm	perch	sport
chirp	march	north

Alphabetical Order

1. _____

2. _____

3. _____

4. _____

5. _____

6. _____

Sentences

1. _____

2. _____

3. _____

R-Controlled Vowels

Overview

Vowel-R Combinations –air and –are

Vowel-r combinations are vowels that are followed by an r and are influenced by the /r/ sound to some degree. In the vowel-r combinations –air and –are, you can hear the long a sound and the /r/ sound. When you say chair and blare, you can hear the influence of r on the vowel sound. This week, students will study more examples of these combinations.

Introduction

Directions: Listen as the words are read aloud slowly. Tap the table for each sound you hear. Talk about how many sounds are in each word. Then, write the words.

chair   stare   fair

glare   hair

1. _____

2. _____

3. _____

4. _____

5. _____

Name: _____ Date: _____

Identification

Directions: Highlight or circle the letters that make the vowel-*r* combinations. Then, read the words aloud.

hare	hairy	**bare**	**fare**	lair
fair	stare	**fairy**	**glare**	square
air	**blare**	hair	pair	**dare**
chair	**stair**	care	snare	**dairy**

Try This!

Find two words above that sound the same but are spelled differently. Fold a sheet of paper in half. On each half, write the word and its definition. Then, draw a picture to show the meaning of each word.

Word Sort

Directions: Read the words in the Word Bank. Sort the words by vowel-*r* combinations. Write them in the chart.

Word Bank

air	fair	repair	square
blare	hair	scare	stair
care	pair	share	stare
dare	rare	snare	

–air	
–are	

Name: _____ Date: _____

Word Play

Directions: Read and solve each word puzzle.

1. chair – ch + st = _____

2. care – c + b = _____

3. stare – are + air = _____

4. rare – r + sn = _____

5. hare – are + air = _____

6. p + air = _____

7. fair – air + are = _____

8. square – qu + t = _____

9. lair – l + ch = _____

10. glare – g + b = _____

Try This!

Choose five words above. Read each word to a friend. Have your friend tap the sounds in the words. Then, switch roles.

Reading

Directions: Read the sentences aloud. Circle the *-air* and *-are* combinations in the sentences. Write these words.

1. The hare ran through the grass and down the hole. _____

2. When playing tag at recess, please play fair! _____

3. She sits in the chair and does her work. _____

4. Do not stare at the sun because it will hurt your eyes. _____

5. There is a glare on the TV when the sun shines through the window.

   _____

6. The girl likes to brush her hair. _____

7. The school nurse takes care of us. _____

8. Carlos can fly the plane through the air. _____

9. That movie gave me a scare! _____

10. I put my tooth under my pillow for the tooth fairy. _____

Try This!

Write a story using some of the words above. Read your story to a friend.

Vowel-R Combinations *-air, -are*

Name: _____ Date: _____

Writing

Directions: Write four sentences with words that have vowel-*r* combinations. Be sure each sentence begins with a capital letter and ends with a punctuation mark.

1. _____

2. _____

3. _____

4. _____

Try This!

Read your sentences to a friend. Have your friend read their sentences to you. Write the sentences your friend reads to you.

1. _____

2. _____

3. _____

4. _____

Vowel–R Combinations –air, –are

Overview

Vowel-R Combinations –eer and –ear

Vowel-*r* combinations are vowels that are followed by an *r* and are influenced by the /r/ sound to some degree. In the vowel-*r* combinations –*eer* and –*ear*, you can hear the long *e* sound and the /r/ sound. When you say *tear* (as in *teardrop*) and *cheer*, you can hear the influence of *r* on the vowel sounds. This week, students will learn about words with these combinations.

Introduction

Directions: Listen closely as the words below are read aloud. Talk about the long *e* sound before the *r* in the words. Then, draw a box around the vowel-*r* combinations.

dear   tear   cheer

fear   steer

Name: _____ Date: _____

Identification

Directions: Read the words in the Word Bank. Underline the letters that make the *–eer* or *–ear* combination in each word. Write the words next to the matching pictures.

Word Bank

| cheer | clear | deer | gear | hear | steer |

 1. _____

 4. _____

 2. _____

 5. _____

 3. _____

 6. _____

Try This!

Use letter tiles or magnets to build words with vowel-*r* combinations. Write five of them.

_____ _____ _____ _____ _____

Word Sort

Directions: Read the words in the Word Bank. Sort the words by vowel-*r* combinations. Write them in the chart.

Word Bank

cheer	fear	rear	spear
clear	gear	sheer	steer
dear	hear	smear	veer
deer	jeer	sneer	year

–eer	
–ear	

Vowel-R Combinations –eer, –ear

Name: _____   Date: _____

Word Play

Directions: Read each word chain. Highlight or circle the letters that change. Underline the words with *–eer* and *–ear*.

jeer → veer → cheer → chair → pair

tear → dear → deer → sheer → steer

stair → stare → steer → sneer → snare

spear → smear → hear → hare → dare

square → stare → rare → rear → fear

Try This!

Look up the meanings of the words *deer* and *dear*. Fold a sheet of paper in half. On the left side, draw a picture to show the meaning of one of the words. On the right side, draw a picture to show the meaning of the other word.

Reading

Directions: Read the letter. Highlight or circle the words with *–eer* and *–ear* patterns. There are seven different words.

Dear Gram and Pop,

I have had the best time at cheer camp! There are so many things to do here. I have made lots of new friends who also love to cheer. We practice each day. We work hard, but we also make time for fun!

In the morning, we get our gear ready. I have pom-poms, sneakers, and a matching top and skirt. My friends and I walk together to the gym, where we spend the morning learning new things. We must listen to our coach and what she tells us to do. One new thing I learned is that you must clear the mat when others are doing jumps and flips. We have to make sure no one gets hurt!

After we practice, we put our gear in the rear of the gym. We have lunch and chit-chat with one another. My new friend Sasha lives near my house! I am happy to have her as a friend.

I hope to come to cheer camp again next year! I cannot wait to show you my routines and introduce you to my new friends. They are so dear to me! I miss you very much and hope you will write me soon.

Love,
Patty

Vowel–R Combinations *–eer, –ear*

Try This!

Write a letter to a friend or family member about something you enjoy. Read your letter to a friend.

Name: _____   Date: _____

Writing

Directions: Use the words in the Word Bank to complete the sentences.

Word Bank

| beard | clear | ears | near | steer |
| cheer | deer | fear | shear | year |

1. Maya loves to sing and spread holiday _____.

2. The _____ ate all my plants!

3. I am in second grade, but next _____ I will be in third grade.

4. The summer is _____!

5. His _____ is long, curly, and white.

6. The farmer needs to _____ his sheep because their coats are long.

7. Do not drink the water if it is not _____.

8. There was _____ in the room during the scary movie.

9. _____ the truck in the right direction.

10. I can pierce my _____ when I turn 10 years old.

Overview

Vowel-R Combinations –our, –ore, and –ure

Similar to vowel-r combinations with *a* and *e*, vowels *u* and *o* form vowel-r combinations when followed by an *r*. You can hear how the *r* is a strong influence over the vowel sound in the words *court*, *more*, and *cure*. This week, students will learn more about the vowel-r combinations –*our*, –*ore*, and –*ure*.

Introduction

Directions: Listen closely as the words are read aloud. Talk about how these words make one /or/ sound. Notice the difference in the word *sure*. Then, draw a box around the vowel-r combinations.

store   your   sure

pour   more

Name: _____ Date: _____

Identification

Directions: Read the words. Circle the *-our* words in blue. Circle the *-ore* words in green. Circle the *-ure* words in red.

pure   four   cure   explore   **your**

chore   ignore   **store**   **mourn**   court

snore   **wore**   **score**   injure   sore

before   shore   treasure   **pour**   **bore**

Try This!

Highlight or circle a word above that you do not know. Use the internet or a dictionary to find its definition. Write the definition, and draw a picture.

_____

_____

_____

Word Sort

Directions: Read the words in the Word Bank. Sort the words by vowel-*r* combinations. Write them in the chart.

Word Bank

bore	ensure	injure	pure
chore	explore	more	score
course	four	mourn	shore
cure	gourd	pour	source

–our	
–ore	
–ure	

Try This!

Write each word from the Word Bank on a note card. Place the note cards around the room. Ask a friend to find the words. Read the words, and sort them a different way.

Name: _____ Date: _____

Word Play

Directions: Read the words in the Word Bank. Highlight or circle the words in the word search.

O	B	S	O	U	R	C	E	P	J
Y	E	Q	C	U	R	E	S	K	F
L	F	O	M	K	W	S	C	F	U
N	O	S	L	O	G	N	O	H	V
C	R	E	I	P	U	O	R	E	Z
C	E	R	W	O	N	R	E	N	G
O	A	V	X	U	P	E	N	D	F
U	F	O	U	R	T	H	F	U	D
R	D	N	O	C	W	P	B	R	L
T	I	L	I	K	K	U	W	E	J

Word Bank

before	cure	fourth	pour	snore
court	endure	mourn	score	source

Reading

Directions: Read the letter. Highlight or circle words with *–our*, *–ore*, and *–ure* combinations. There are seven different words.

Dear Grandma,

I'm excited to see you for the holidays! I have been so good this year! I did my best to be as good as I could be. I took very good care of my little sister Eva, and I made sure to play fair.

Dad and I went to the store last week to look at some toys. There were so many things I would like to have! First, I would love a science kit. I would put it in my room, and it would be like having my very own science lab! I want to be a scientist when I grow up, so this would help me get ready. With science, there are so many great things to explore!

My sister is too little to write you a note, so I want to share what she wants for the holidays. She loves it when our family goes to the shore in the summer, so she would like some toys to play with in the sand. She will start playing soccer, so some gear to get her started would be great. I can't wait to watch her score! My friends say being a big brother is a bore, but I don't think so.

I also wanted to say thank you. You do a lot to ensure that our family has a great holiday, and you are awesome for doing so. I will write you again soon!

Love,
Remy

Vowel-R Combinations *–our*, *–ore*, *–ure*

Name: _____ Date: _____

Writing

Directions: Read the words in the Word Bank. Choose five words, and write them in sentences. Be sure each sentence begins with a capital letter and ends with a punctuation mark.

Word Bank

chore	cure	fourth	mourn	score
course	explore	injure	pure	store

1. _____

2. _____

3. _____

4. _____

5. _____

Try This!

Look around the room. Find two other things that have vowel-*r* combinations in their names. Write the names of the objects.

_____ _____

Vowel-*R* Combinations –our, –ore, –ure

Overview

Inflectional Endings –s, –es, and –ies

Inflectional endings change the meaning of a base word. When added to a noun, the –s, –es, and –ies inflectional endings all mean "more than one." For example, the word *cat* means one cat, but the word *cats* refers to more than one cat. Depending on the base word, the –s inflectional ending can sound like /s/ or /z/.

You use the inflectional ending –es when a base word ends in s, x, z, or consonant digraphs *sh* or *ch*. For example, the word *dish* becomes *dishes*. When a word ends in a y, you drop the y and add –ies. For example, the word *baby* becomes *babies*.

Introduction

Directions: The words below are changed to be plural, or more than one. Highlight or circle the letters that are changed or added. The first one has been done for you. Talk about which words only add an –s and which add –es or –ies.

1. lad(y) → lad(ies)

2. wish → wishes

3. dog → dogs

4. stop → stops

5. catch → catches

6. fly → flies

Most words only add an –s when they become plural. Add -es when a base word ends in s, x, or z. You also add -es when a base word ends in digraphs *sh* or *ch*.

Name: _____ Date: _____

Identification

Directions: Circle the letters that make the –s, –es, and –ies endings in the words. Then, read the words aloud.

socks   classes   clicks   coats   **flies**

bugs   babies   trees   **buzzes**   clouds

sleeps   benches   **wishes**   bees   witches

stories   **ties**   swings   sheets   **spies**

Try This!

Write the words above on craft sticks. Write "Oh, no!" on a few more craft sticks. Put all the craft sticks into a cup. Take turns with a friend picking a craft stick and reading the word. If you choose an "Oh, no!" stick, return all your words to the cup.

Word Sort

Directions: Read the words. Add the –s, –es, or –ies inflectional endings. Then, sort the words into the chart.

1. bag _____

2. bench _____

3. class _____

4. fry _____

5. story _____

6. slide _____

7. tree _____

8. glass _____

9. table _____

10. spy _____

11. sheet _____

12. wish _____

–s	
–es	
–ies	

Inflectional Endings –s, –es, –ies

Name: _____ Date: _____

Word Play

Directions: Underline the final consonant sound in each base word. Add −s, −es, or −ies to make the word plural. Write the new word.

1. coat + _____ = _____

2. dish + _____ = _____

3. light + _____ = _____

4. fly + _____ = _____

5. catch + _____ = _____

6. fish + _____ = _____

7. lady + _____ = _____

8. chair + _____ = _____

9. story + _____ = _____

10. baby + _____ = _____

Try This!

Choose four words above. Write two sentences using two of the words in each sentence.

_____

_____

Reading

Directions: Read the passage. Circle nouns with the inflectional endings *–s, –es,* and *–ies*. There are six different words. Then, draw pictures to match the steps in the butterfly life cycle.

Butterfly Life Cycle

Butterflies have an interesting life cycle. Every butterfly begins as an egg. A young caterpillar hatches from the egg. The caterpillar spends most of its time eating and growing. It munches on leaves, grasses, and other plants. Once the little bug is big enough, it forms a chrysalis. Then, an amazing change takes place. After a while, the butterfly breaks free from the chrysalis and stretches its new wings. It is ready to enter the world! It flies to different flowers to drink their sweet nectar. When the butterfly is ready, it will lay its eggs. Then, the life cycle begins again!

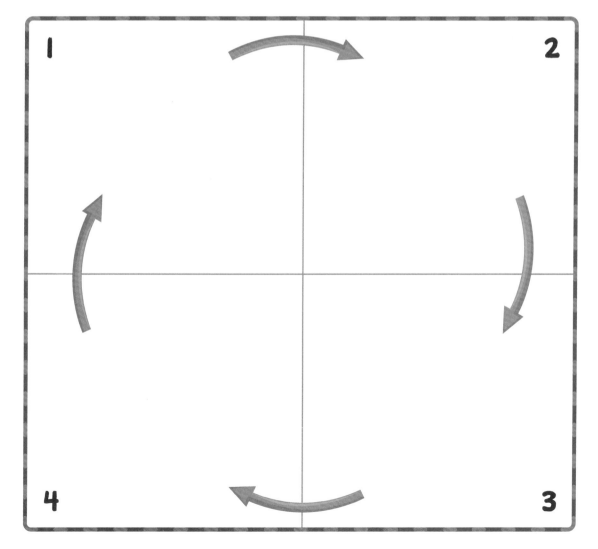

Inflectional Endings –s, –es, –ies

Name: _____ Date: _____

Writing

Directions: Write the words from the Word Bank in alphabetical order. Then, choose three words, and write them in sentences. Be sure each sentence begins with a capital letter and ends with a punctuation mark.

Inflectional Endings –s, –es, –ies

Word Bank

| benches | glasses | dishes |
| swings | stories | blankets |

Alphabetical Order

1. _____

2. _____

3. _____

4. _____

5. _____

6. _____

Sentences

1. _____

2. _____

3. _____

Overview

Inflectional Ending –ing

Inflectional endings change the meaning of a base word. The –ing inflectional ending means that an action is happening right now. For example, the word *jumping* means that someone or something is jumping right now.

When a one-syllable word ends in a single consonant with a short vowel, the consonant is doubled before adding –ing. For example, the word *grab* is a one-syllable word that ends in a single consonant (*b*). So, the word *grab* becomes *grabbing*.

When a word ends in an *e*, the *e* is dropped and replaced with the inflectional ending –ing. For example, the word *make* becomes *making*.

Introduction

Directions: Add –ing to each of the words below. Use the rules in the box below to help you. Talk about how the words were changed.

1. fish ⟶ _____

2. skip ⟶ _____

3. rake ⟶ _____

4. stop ⟶ _____

5. land ⟶ _____

6. hide ⟶ _____

When a word ends in *e*, drop the *e* to add –ing.

Example: *shake* becomes *shaking*

Double the consonant when:

- the word is one syllable,
- it ends in a single consonant,
- and it has a short vowel.

Example: *flip* becomes *flipping*

Name: _____   Date: _____

Identification

Directions: Circle the letters that make the –*ing* endings. Then, write the base words.

1. skipping   _____

2. hanging   _____

3. swinging   _____

4. running   _____

5. baking   _____

6. catching   _____

7. humming   _____

8. riding   _____

9. making   _____

10. writing   _____

Try This!

Play a game of charades with friends. Act out a word from this page. Have your friends guess which word you act out. Then, switch roles.

Word Sort

Directions: Read the words. Add the *-ing* inflectional ending to each word. Then, sort the words into the chart.

1. bake _____

2. catch _____

3. drive _____

4. end _____

5. fade _____

6. push _____

7. ring _____

8. run _____

9. skip _____

10. write _____

Add *-ing*	
Double Final Consonant, Add *-ing*	
Drop the *e*, Add *-ing*	

Try This!

Write the words from the chart on note cards. Sort the words differently. Get creative!

Name: _____ Date: _____

Word Play

Directions: Add the suffix *–ing* to each word. Write the new word, and read it aloud.

1. write + ing = _____

2. swing + ing = _____

3. skip + ing = _____

4. push + ing = _____

5. jump + ing = _____

6. bake + ing = _____

7. make + ing = _____

8. run + ing = _____

9. drive + ing = _____

10. golf + ing = _____

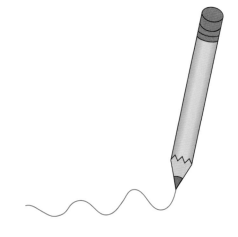

Try This!

Make your own word puzzle for a friend.

_____ + ing = _____

Reading

Directions: Read the poem. Circle words with the *–ing* inflectional ending. There are seven different words.

Spring Changes

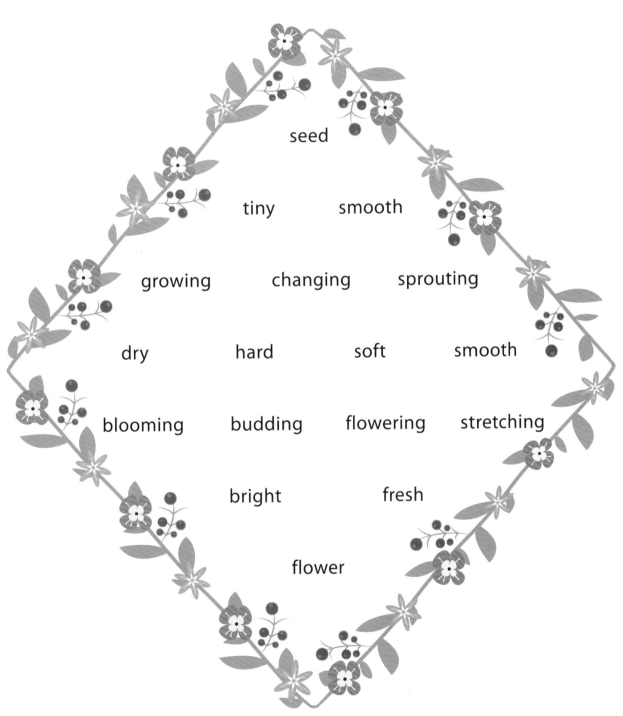

seed

tiny   smooth

growing   changing   sprouting

dry   hard   soft   smooth

blooming   budding   flowering   stretching

bright   fresh

flower

Inflectional Ending –ing

Writing

Directions: Write four sentences with words that have the *–ing* ending. Be sure each sentence begins with a capital letter and ends with a punctuation mark.

1. _____

2. _____

3. _____

4. _____

Try This!

Read your sentences to a friend. Have your friend read their sentences to you. Write the sentences your friend reads to you.

1. _____

2. _____

3. _____

4. _____

Inflectional Ending –ing

Overview

Inflectional Ending –ed

Inflectional endings change the meaning of a base word. The –ed inflectional ending means that an action happened in the past. For example, the word *jumped* means that someone or something already did the action of jumping.

When a one-syllable word ends in a single consonant with a short vowel, the consonant is doubled before adding –ed. For example, the word *grab* is a one-syllable word that ends in a single consonant (*b*). *Grab* becomes *grabbed*. When a word ends in an *e*, only a *d* is added. For example, the word *rake* becomes *raked*.

The –ed ending is pronounced differently depending on the ending of the base word.

Introduction

Directions: Add –ed to each of the words below. Use the rules in the box below to help you. Talk about how the words were changed.

1. act → _____   **4.** love → _____

2. wave → _____   **5.** dump → _____

3. stop → _____   **6.** drop → _____

> When a word ends in *e*, only add a *d*.
> **Example:** *save* becomes *saved*
>
> Double the consonant when:
> - the word is one syllable,
> - it ends in a single consonant,
> - and it has a short vowel.
>
> **Example:** *hop* becomes *hopped*

Name: _____ Date: _____

Identification

Directions: Read the words. Circle the sound the *-ed* ending represents (/t/, /d/, or /id/).

1. zoomed /t/ /d/ /id/   9. liked /t/ /d/ /id/

2. helped /t/ /d/ /id/   10. mashed /t/ /d/ /id/

3. looked /t/ /d/ /id/   11. barked /t/ /d/ /id/

4. baked /t/ /d/ /id/   12. jumped /t/ /d/ /id/

5. dusted /t/ /d/ /id/   13. ended /t/ /d/ /id/

6. landed /t/ /d/ /id/   14. weeded /t/ /d/ /id/

7. sailed /t/ /d/ /id/   15. played /t/ /d/ /id/

8. yawned /t/ /d/ /id/   16. mailed /t/ /d/ /id/

Try This!

Search a book. List three other words with the inflectional ending *-ed*.

_____ _____ _____

Word Sort

Directions: Read the words. Add the *–ed* inflectional endings. Then, sort the words based on their *–ed* sounds /t/, /d/, or /id/.

1. bark _____

2. bike _____

3. fish _____

4. hand _____

5. jot _____

6. lick _____

7. live _____

8. park _____

9. sail _____

10. zoom _____

/t/	
/d/	
/id/	

Name: _____ Date: _____

Word Play

Directions: Add the suffix *–ed* to each word. Write the new word, and read it aloud.

I. rush + ed = _____

2. toss + ed = _____

3. boom + ed = _____

4. rain + ed = _____

5. sail + ed = _____

6. landing – ing + ed = _____

7. jumping – ing + ed = _____

8. rushing – ing + ed = _____

9. waving – ing + ed = _____

10. hiking – ing + ed = _____

Try This!

Write the words above on craft sticks. Write "Oh, no!" on a few more craft sticks. Put all the craft sticks into a cup. Take turns with a friend picking a craft stick and reading the word. If you choose an "Oh, no!" stick, return all your words back to the cup.

Reading

Directions: Read the letter. Circle words with the *-ed* ending. There are nine different words.

Dear Pop,

Thank you for coming to my birthday party. I had the best time, and it was so nice of you to be there. Thank you so much for the race cars you gave me for my birthday gift. I enjoyed playing with them at my party! All my friends thought they were so cool. After the party, my friends slept over at my house. We played with the race cars all night long! We made a racetrack around the house. The cars zipped through the halls and zoomed from room to room. They sped down the stairs and crashed into the front door! (They were not damaged, though!) I wanted to keep playing with them, but Mom said it was time for bed. I think we were making too much noise.

I had hoped that my birthday would be fun, and it ended up being a blast! Thank you for being so kind and for giving me such a great gift! I know the next time my friends come over, we will make a new racetrack, just like we did the night of my party. It will be amazing!

Love always,
Jack

Name: _____ Date: _____

Writing

Directions: Read the words in the Word Bank. Choose five words, and write them in sentences. Be sure each sentence begins with a capital letter and ends with a punctuation mark.

Inflectional Ending –ed

Word Bank

barked	closed	helped	named	picked
boomed	ended	landed	pawed	rained

1. _____

2. _____

3. _____

4. _____

5. _____

Try This!

Write a short poem using some of the words in the Word Bank. Read your poem to a friend.

_____

_____

_____

_____

Overview

Syllable Patterns
VC/CV and VCCCV

When dividing words into syllables, always begin by marking the vowel sounds. Then, look at the number of consonants between the vowels. Knowing syllabication patterns will help you determine where to divide the word.

The VC/CV syllabication pattern splits the syllables between consonants. For example, the word *rabbit* has two vowels with two consonants between them. The word is split *rab-bit*.

The VCCCV syllabication pattern can be split after the first or second consonant. It is important not to split consonant blends or consonant digraphs. For example, the word *pumpkin* is split *pump-kin* because you do not want to separate the *–mp* consonant blend. However, the word *monster* is split *mon-ster* because you do not want to separate the *st* consonant blend.

Compound words are always divided into two smaller words.

Introduction

Directions: Listen to the words as they are read aloud. Mark the vowels with a *V*. Mark the consonants with a *C*. Then, mark where to split the words. The first one has been done for you.

nut/meg   magnet   subtract   sandwich
V C   C V

Name: _____ Date: _____

Identification

Directions: Write a *V* under each vowel and a *C* under each consonant. Circle the syllable pattern. Divide the words, and read them aloud.

Syllable Patterns

1. sunset   VC/CV   VC/CCV   VCC/CV

2. **rabbit**   VC/CV   VC/CCV   VCC/CV

3. **monster**   VC/CV   VC/CCV   VCC/CV

4. pencil   VC/CV   VC/CCV   VCC/CV

5. **mushroom**   VC/CV   VC/CCV   VCC/CV

6. sudden   VC/CV   VC/CCV   VCC/CV

7. **kitten**   VC/CV   VC/CCV   VCC/CV

8. **hundred**   VC/CV   VC/CCV   VCC/CV

9. napkin   VC/CV   VC/CCV   VCC/CV

10. subtract   VC/CV   VC/CCV   VCC/CV

Try This!

Write five words on note cards. Swap your note cards with a friend. Cut each word where it should be split. Mix up your cut note cards, and try to piece the words together like a puzzle.

Word Sort

Directions: Read the words. Divide the words, and write the syllables. Then, sort the words based on the syllable pattern.

1. athlete _____ _____

2. dentist _____ _____

3. gossip _____ _____

4. dolphin _____ _____

5. hundred _____ _____

6. insect _____ _____

7. partner _____ _____

8. sandwich _____ _____

9. tennis _____ _____

10. trumpet _____ _____

Syllable Patterns

VC/CV	
VC/CCV	
VCC/CV	

Name: _____ Date: _____

Word Play

Directions: Look at the pictures. Write the missing syllables to complete the words.

 sun _____

 _____ plode

 den_____

 cac _____

 _____ tract

 _____ ten

 _____ kin

 _____ ster

 in _____

 chil _____

Reading

Directions: Read the sentences aloud. Circle the VCCV and VCCCV words in the sentences. Write the words you circled.

1. The rabbit ran through the woods. _____

2. To get ready for the test, make sure your pencil is sharp. _____

3. It will snow a lot this winter. _____

4. The dentist will make sure my teeth are clean. _____

5. We went to the pumpkin patch to pick the best one. _____

6. The doctor will see you soon. _____

7. My birthday was the best one yet! _____

8. The insect flew around the trees. _____

9. The kitten slept close to its mother. _____

10. Are you afraid of monsters in the dark? _____

Syllable Patterns

Name: _____   Date: _____

Writing

Directions: Use the words in the Word Bank to complete the sentences.

Word Bank

| bathroom | conflict | letter | subtract | trumpet |
| complete | dolphin | monster | sunset | winter |

Syllable Patterns

1. When I was little, I thought there was a _____ under my bed.

2. I learn to _____ big numbers in math class.

3. I saw a _____ jump out of the water at the beach.

4. I hope to learn to play the _____ in fourth grade!

5. The best season is _____ because it is fun to play in the snow.

6. My brother writes me a _____ from camp each summer.

7. I saw the _____ each evening on my trip.

8. I will turn in my homework when it is _____.

9. I hope my plans do not have a _____ this weekend.

10. The _____ door is squeaky.

Overview

Syllable Patterns
V/CV and VC/V

When dividing words into syllables, always begin by marking the vowel sounds. Then, look at the number of consonants between the vowels. Knowing syllabication patterns will help you determine where to divide the word.

The VCV syllabication pattern can be split before or after the consonant. When the word is divided before the consonant, it leaves the vowel in the first syllable open. For example, in *music*, the *u* is a long *u* sound, so the word is split *mu/sic*. In the word *comet*, the *o* is short, so it must be divided after the consonant to make the vowel short. The word is split *com/et*.

Introduction

Directions: Listen to the words as they are read aloud. Mark the vowels with a *V*. Mark the consonants with a *C*. Then, mark where to split the words. The first one has been done for you.

rob/in   melon   seven   frozen
V C V

Name: _____ Date: _____

Identification

Directions: Write a *V* under each vowel and a *C* under each consonant. Circle the syllable pattern. Divide the words, and read them aloud.

1. lemon   V/CV   VC/V

2. **cabin**   V/CV   VC/V

3. river   V/CV   VC/V

4. paper   V/CV   VC/V

5. **robot**   V/CV   VC/V

6. music   V/CV   VC/V

7. tiger   V/CV   VC/V

Try This!

8. even   V/CV   VC/V

Have a friend read five of the words from this page to you. Clap the syllables in each word. Then, tap the sounds in each syllable. Use what you know about sounds to spell the syllables. Then, write the whole word.

9. **robin**   V/CV   VC/V

10. protect   V/CV   VC/V

Word Sort

Directions: Read the words. Divide the words, and write the syllables. Then, sort the words based on the syllable pattern.

1. basic   _____   _____

2. cabin   _____   _____

3. diner   _____   _____

4. hotel   _____   _____

5. planet   _____   _____

6. present   _____   _____

7. river   _____   _____

8. salad   _____   _____

9. second   _____   _____

10. talent   _____   _____

V/CV	
VC/V	

Name: _____ Date: _____

Word Play

Directions: Read each clue. Complete the crossword puzzle.

Down

1. someone who flies a plane
2. a special skill
4. a bird with a red chest
6. the number that comes after six
8. a sour yellow fruit

Across

3. a flower that blooms in spring
5. the opposite of closed
7. an animal with orange and black stripes
9. the opposite of odd
10. a place to stay on vacation

Reading

Directions: Read the poem. Circle the words with VCCV, VCCCV, and VCV patterns. Write the words you circled, and divide them into syllables.

Leaves

Fly, flutter, drift, spin,

Falling downward, softly, crunch,

Empty twigs remain.

1. _____

2. _____

3. _____

4. _____

5. _____

6. _____

Name: _____   Date: _____

Writing

Directions: Write four sentences. Use at least one two-syllable word in each sentence. Be sure each sentence begins with a capital letter and ends with a punctuation mark.

1. _____

2. _____

3. _____

4. _____

Try This!

Read your sentences to a friend. Have your friend read their sentences to you. Write the sentences your friend reads to you.

1. _____

2. _____

3. _____

4. _____

Overview

Consonant +*le*

When a multisyllabic word ends in a consonant followed by the /l/ sound, it is spelled –*le*. The –*le* is its own syllable. For example, the word *table* has four sounds: /t/ /ā/ /b/ /l/. And it has two syllables: *ta/ble*. The final /l/ sound is spelled –*le* because it follows a consonant at the end of the word. Students will explore this pattern further this week.

Introduction

Directions: Look at the words below. Say them aloud. Notice that each word has two syllables. The –*le* is always its own syllable. Draw a slash in each word to divide it into syllables. The first one has been done for you.

rid/dle   bottle   angle   candle

Name: _____ **Date:** _____

Identification

Directions: Read the words aloud. Draw sound boxes around each word.

Example: table

t	a	b	le

1. j u n g l e

2. a p p l e

3. s i m p l e

4. t i c k l e

5. a b l e

6. c a n d l e

7. s h u f f l e

8. p u r p l e

9. c r u m p l e

10. t u r t l e

Try This!

Look around the room. Find two other things that have a consonant +*le* in their names. Write the names of the objects.

_____ _____

Word Sort

Directions: Read the words in the Word Bank. Sort the words based on the syllable pattern.

Word Bank

able	partner	robot	snuggle
apple	penny	second	subway
doodle	railroad	seven	talent
giggle	ripple	simple	turtle

Consonant +*le*	
Other Two-Syllable Words	

Try This!

Write two other words that have two syllables.

_____ _____

Name: _____ Date: _____

Word Play

Directions: Use the letters to make words with the consonant +*le* pattern. Then, choose three words, and use them in sentences. Be sure each sentence begins with a capital letter and ends with a punctuation mark.

l	e	u	i	c	k
p	b	a	m	s	t

Consonant +*le*

Words

1. _____   5. _____

2. _____   6. _____

3. _____   7. _____

4. _____   8. _____

Sentences

1. _____

2. _____

3. _____

Reading

Directions: Read the sentences aloud. Circle the consonant +*le* words in the sentences. Write the words you circled.

1. Buckle your seatbelt before you begin driving. _____

2. The doodle is of a very silly kitten. _____

3. The purple flowers will bloom in the spring. _____

4. We plant apple seeds every fall. _____

5. Drake will light the candle for those he loves. _____

6. The duck waddles back to the pond to swim. _____

7. What animals live in the jungle? _____

8. My puppy likes to snuggle at bedtime. _____

9. Shuffle the deck of cards before we play. _____

10. Give the warm bottle to the baby. _____

Consonant +*le*

Name: _____   Date: _____

Writing

Directions: Write the words from the Word Bank in alphabetical order. Then, choose three words, and write them in sentences. Be sure each sentence begins with a capital letter and ends with a punctuation mark.

Word Bank

table	pickle	jungle
candle	crumple	puzzle

Alphabetical Order

1. _____

2. _____

3. _____

4. _____

5. _____

6. _____

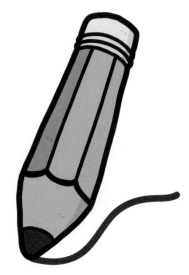

Sentences

1. _____

2. _____

3. _____

Overview

Prefixes *un–* and *im–*

Just like a suffix, a prefix is under the umbrella term *affix*. An affix is the smallest unit of sound in a word that carries meaning. A prefix comes at the beginning of a word and changes the meaning of the base word.

The prefixes *un–* and *im–* both mean "not." This week, students will study words with these prefixes.

Introduction

Directions: Add the prefix *un–* to the beginning of each word. Write the new words. Talk about the meanings of the new words.

fair _____

lucky _____

tie _____

Directions: Add the prefix *im–* to the beginning of each word. Write the new words. Talk about the meanings of the new words.

polite _____

perfect _____

possible _____

Name: _____ Date: _____

Identification

Directions: Circle the prefixes. Read the words. Write the meanings of the words.

1. uncap _____

2. **unfair** _____

3. impossible _____

4. unclear _____

5. **immature** _____

6. imperfect _____

7. **impolite** _____

8. impure _____

9. **unfold** _____

10. unkind _____

Try This!

Search a book. List at least five other words with prefixes *un–* and *im–*.

_____

_____

Word Sort

Directions: Read each phrase. Decide whether you would use *un–* or *im–* as a prefix. Write the new word. Then, write the words in the chart.

1. to not be clear   _____

2. to not be even   _____

3. to not be lucky   _____

4. to not be perfect   _____

5. to not be polite   _____

6. to not be possible   _____

7. to not be safe   _____

8. to not be tidy   _____

9. to not be true   _____

10. to not like   _____

11. to not pack   _____

12. to not roll   _____

un–	
im–	

Name: _____   Date: _____

Word Play

Directions: Read the words in the Word Bank. Highlight or circle the words in the word search.

```
A   H   L   X   U   N   L   O   A   D
N   I   M   P   E   R   F   E   C   T
I   U   N   R   O   L   L   U   D   U
I   M   N   M   M   J   F   N   U   N
U   M   P   C   O   M   E   W   N   F
N   Y   P   O   L   O   A   I   S   A
K   D   R   U   L   E   Z   N   C   I
I   A   N   Q   R   I   A   D   R   R
N   I   W   Z   V   E   T   R   E   S
D   R   O   V   S   M   X   E   W   V
```

Word Bank

imperfect	impure	unfair	unload	unscrew
impolite	unclear	unkind	unroll	unwind

Name: _____ Date: _____

Reading

Directions: Read the passage aloud. Circle the words with *im–* and *un–* prefixes. There are eight different words.

Morning Routines

Every morning, I get ready for school. I make my bed, even though I don't like to. But my dad says it's best to not be untidy. I take my clothes into the bathroom. I take a shower, brush my teeth, and get dressed. Then, my dad helps me brush my hair, and we go to the kitchen for breakfast. I make sure my homework is in my backpack. I put on my shoes, coat, and backpack. I hop in the car, and Dad drives me to school.

I enter the school and walk to my classroom. When I get there, my teacher, Miss Green, welcomes me to the classroom.

I find my seat and unpack my backpack. I put my homework in the bin. Then, I have a few minutes of free play to unwind. I unplug my laptop from the cart and work on my online reading. When all my friends arrive, we are ready for morning meeting.

Miss Green reminds us of our classroom rules. We need to make sure we are not being unkind or unjust. We talk about what is impolite and what we can do to be fair. Kindness is important at my school! We all share ways that we can be kind to one another. Then, I head to my seat and grab my dry erase board, marker, and eraser. I uncap my marker, and I am ready. The morning is off to a great start!

Prefixes *un–, im–*

WEEK 32 DAY 4

© Shell Education   130214—180 Days™: Phonics   201

Name: _____ Date: _____

Writing

Directions: Write four sentences with words that have prefixes. Be sure each sentence begins with a capital letter and ends with a punctuation mark.

1. _____

2. _____

3. _____

4. _____

Try This!

Read your sentences to a friend. Have your friend read their sentences to you. Write the sentences your friend reads to you.

1. _____

2. _____

3. _____

4. _____

Overview

Prefixes *re–* and *dis–*

Just like a suffix, a prefix is under the umbrella term *affix*. An affix is the smallest unit of sound in a word that carries meaning. A prefix comes at the beginning of a word and changes the meaning of the base word.

The prefix *re–* means to do something again. The prefix *dis–* means the opposite of something. This week, students will study words with these prefixes.

Introduction

Directions: Add the prefix *re–* to the beginning of each word. Write the new words. Talk about the meanings of the new words.

copy   _____

make   _____

pack   _____

Directions: Add the prefix *dis–* to the beginning of each word. Write the new words. Talk about the meanings of the new words.

like   _____

trust   _____

please   _____

Name: _____ Date: _____

Identification

Directions: Circle the prefixes. Read the words. Write the meanings of the words.

1. recall _____

2. **repack** _____

3. repay _____

4. reread _____

5. **retell** _____

6. dislike _____

7. **distrust** _____

8. displace _____

9. **displease** _____

10. distaste _____

Try This!

Search a book. List three other words with prefixes *re-* or *dis-*.

_____ _____ _____

Word Sort

Directions: Read the words in the Word Bank. Sort the words based on their meanings.

Word Bank

rewrite	reread	rewind	displease
dislike	distrust	replace	repay
disobey	return	distaste	discomfort
rewash	repack	recycle	recall

to do again	
the opposite of	

Prefixes *re−*, *dis−*

Name: _____ Date: _____

Word Play

Directions: Add the prefix to each word. Write the new word, and read it aloud. Then, write the new word's meaning.

Prefixes re–, dis–

1. re + cycle = _____

   Meaning: _____

2. re + wrap = _____

   Meaning: _____

3. re + write = _____

   Meaning: _____

4. dis + like = _____

   Meaning: _____

5. dis + trust = _____

   Meaning: _____

6. dis + taste = _____

   Meaning: _____

7. re + pay = _____

   Meaning: _____

8. re + name = _____

   Meaning: _____

9. re + tell = _____

   Meaning: _____

130214—180 Days™: Phonics

Reading

Directions: Read the sentences aloud. Circle words with *re–* and *dis–* prefixes. Write the words you circled.

I. Sitting for too long can cause discomfort.

_____

2. You do not want to displease your principal.

_____

3. If you cannot remember the story, reread it.

_____

4. I need to reheat my dinner because it is too cold.

_____

5. I need to recopy my homework because it is too messy.

_____

6. I broke my arm and will need to rewrap my bandage.

_____

7. Marsha needs to rewrite the story so that it makes sense.

_____

8. Tyrone will retype his report with the new edits.

_____

9. When cleaning out your desk, discard any trash.

_____

Prefixes *re–, dis–*

Name: _____ Date: _____

Writing

Directions: Read the words in the Word Bank. Choose five words, and write them in sentences. Be sure each sentence begins with a capital letter and ends with a punctuation mark.

Prefixes *re–, dis–*

Word Bank

discard	dislodge	displease	replace	rewind
dislike	displace	distrust	reread	rewrite

1. _____

2. _____

3. _____

4. _____

5. _____

Try This!

Highlight or circle a word you do not know in the Word Bank. Use the internet or a dictionary to find the definition. Write the definition, and draw a picture.

_____

_____

_____

Overview

Suffix –ly

Just like a prefix, a suffix is under the umbrella term *affix*. An affix is the smallest unit of sound in a word that carries meaning. A suffix comes at the end of a word and changes the meaning of the base word.

When the suffix –ly is added to a base word, it describes something as "having the quality of _____." For example, when adding –ly to the word *quick*, the word *quickly* is created, which means "in a quick way" or "having the quality of being quick."

For words that end in y, the final y is changed to an i before adding the suffix –ly. For example, *happy* becomes *happily*.

Introduction

Directions: Circle the suffix in each word. Then, write the base word. Talk about what each word means.

strongly _____

easily _____

strangely _____

gladly _____

hungrily _____

Name: _____ Date: _____

Identification

Directions: Add the suffix –*ly* to each of the words. If the word ends in *y*, change it to an *i* before adding –*ly*. Write the new words.

1. proud + ly = _____

2. glad + ly = _____

3. happy + ly = _____

4. slow + ly = _____

5. love + ly = _____

6. quick + ly = _____

7. loud + ly = _____

8. swift + ly = _____

9. quiet + ly = _____

10. easy + ly = _____

Suffix –ly

Try This!

Play a game of charades. Write the words above on note cards. Take turns acting out the words. Try to guess and describe the actions.

Word Sort

Directions: Read the words. Add the –ly suffix to each word. If the word ends in y, change it to an i before adding –ly. Then, sort the words into the chart.

1. angry _____

2. brave _____

3. bright _____

4. busy _____

5. calm _____

6. happy _____

7. lone _____

8. most _____

9. quick _____

10. sloppy _____

11. strange _____

–ly	
Change y to i and Add –ly	

Suffix –ly

Name: _____   Date: _____

Word Play

Directions: Read each clue. Complete the crossword puzzle.

Suffix –ly

Down

1. to be glad to do something
2. to do something fast
3. to do something in an organized way
4. to do something in a kind way

Across

5. to do something in a gentle way
6. to do something with pride
7. something that is very nice or beautiful
8. to do something with ease
9. to do something with a lot of noise

Reading

Directions: Read the text in the box. Then, read the haiku. Highlight or circle the words with the suffix –*ly*. There are four different words. Then, write your own haiku. Use at least two –*ly* words.

What Is a Haiku?

A haiku is a kind of poem that comes from Japan. It has three lines. The first and last lines each have five syllables. The second line has seven syllables.

The Wind

Softly, gently waves

Strongly and wildly blows

Then calms to a breeze

_____

_____

_____

_____

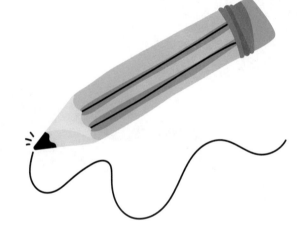

Name: _____   Date: _____

Writing

Directions: Write the words from the Word Bank in alphabetical order. Then, choose three words, and write them in sentences. Be sure each sentence begins with a capital letter and ends with a punctuation mark.

Word Bank

easily	happily	quietly
slowly	sadly	quickly

Suffix –ly

Alphabetical Order

1. _____

2. _____

3. _____

4. _____

5. _____

6. _____

Sentences

1. _____

2. _____

3. _____

Overview

Contractions

A contraction is when two words are shortened into one word using an apostrophe. For example, the words *are not* can be shortened into the contraction *aren't*. Shortening words makes it easier to talk in conversation. Contractions can be identified because they have apostrophes that combine two smaller words into one. This week, students will study contractions and the words that create them.

Introduction

Directions: Study each set of words. These words can come together to make a contraction. To make a contraction, some letters are taken out. They are replaced with an apostrophe. Write each set of words as a contraction. The first one has been done for you.

1. can not _____can't_____

2. I am _____

3. we are _____

4. it is _____

Name: _____ Date: _____

Identification

Directions: Draw lines to match the words to their contractions.

1. I am   it's

2. he is   aren't

3. we are   we're

4. is not   I'll

5. I will   hasn't

6. they are   I'm

7. have not   haven't

8. it is   he's

9. are not   they're

10. has not   isn't

Try This!

Write the words from the left column on note cards. Match and cut cards to form contractions. Add an apostrophe to each contraction.

Word Sort

Directions: Read the words in the Word Bank. Sort the words based on what the base words are being combined with.

Word Bank

aren't	haven't	it's	we're
can't	he's	she's	weren't
don't	I'm	shouldn't	
hasn't	isn't	they're	

Am	
Are	
Not	
Is	

Contractions

Name: _____   Date: _____

Word Play

Directions: Put each set of words together to make a contraction.

1. we + are   = _____

2. have + not   = _____

3. is + not   = _____

4. it + is   = _____

5. has + not   = _____

6. I + am   = _____

7. he + is   = _____

8. they + are   = _____

9. are + not   = _____

10. she + will   = _____

Try This!

Write your own word puzzle. Ask a friend to solve it.

_____ + _____ = _____

Reading

Directions: Read each sentence aloud. Circle the contraction in each sentence. Write the two words that form each contraction.

1. I'm going shopping for food for the week.

   _____ _____

2. Aren't you going to be late for school?

   _____ _____

3. Shreya hasn't had a break in a long time.

   _____ _____

4. We haven't solved the puzzle just yet!

   _____ _____

5. She didn't do the laundry last week.

   _____ _____

6. It isn't time to take Cooper to the vet until the end of the month.

   _____ _____

7. Madison can't play until she finishes her homework.

   _____ _____

8. He's going to the concert with Josiah.

   _____ _____

9. They're going to wake up early in the morning to watch the sunrise.

   _____ _____

10. We're on our way to see the Festival of Lights!

    _____ _____

Name: _____ Date: _____

Writing

Directions: Use the words in the Word Bank to complete the sentences.

Word Bank

aren't	haven't	I'm	it's	they're
hasn't	he's	isn't	she's	we're

1. _____ almost time to prepare for the Holi party.

2. _____ going to unplug the TV to see if he can get it to work again.

3. _____ it a beautiful morning?

4. Why _____ you going to go to the concert tonight?

5. _____ washing the peaches before I eat them.

6. _____ sitting on the benches while we wait for the game to begin.

7. _____ turning four this spring and wants cupcakes for her party.

8. It _____ rained in quite some time.

9. I _____ got a clue what we will do this weekend.

10. _____ humming the tune of the song while they drive.

Contractions

Overview

Cumulative Review

This week, students will review the phonics skills they have learned. By learning the relationships between letters, letter combinations, and the sounds they make, beginning readers can strengthen their reading skills. By breaking words apart, or segmenting, and then blending sounds together, students can apply phonics concepts to new words.

Introduction

Directions: Place counters or coins on the dots. Listen closely as each word is read aloud slowly. Slide the counters into the boxes as you hear sounds in each word. Then, write the letters that stand for each sound in the boxes.

peach

start

broil

Name: _____ Date: _____

Identification

Directions: Look at the pictures. Write the missing letters to complete the words.

 turt _____

 _____ ash

 m _____ se

 lad _____

 ch_____

 r _____ ny

 b _____ k

 _____ ess

 p _____ se

 b _____

Try This!

Draw a picture. Write the word with a sound missing, just like in the activity above. Give your drawing to a friend, and have them fill in the missing sound.

Name: _____ **Date:** _____

Word Sort

Directions: Read the words in the Word Bank. Sort the words into the chart. Start with diphthongs, *r*-controlled vowels, and affixes. Sort the remaining words into the short- and long-vowel categories.

Word Bank

babies	fixes	shadow	thumb
broil	knock	sport	unfit
catch	paint	stoke	waist
cent	repeat	thigh	yellow
dislike	running	thorn	

***R*-Controlled Vowels**	
Diphthongs	
Affixes	
Short Vowels	
Long Vowels	

Cumulative Review

Name: _____ Date: _____

Word Play

Directions: Read each word chain. Highlight or circle the letters that change.

spear → tear → team → gleam → gleams

lad → lamb → limb → climb → climbing

shell → fell → fill → spill → spilled

peach → peaches → beaches → reaches → roaches

sunshine → suntan → sunny → funny → funky

Try This!

Make a word chain. Start with the word *point*. Change one sound at a time. Write your new words.

point→_____ →_____ →_____ →_____

Reading

Directions: Read the recipe aloud. Draw a picture to match the recipe.

Cumulative Review

• Recipe •

Ice Cream Sundae

· · · · · · · · · · · **INGREDIENTS** (serves 4)· · · · · · · · · · ·

- Ice cream (your favorite flavor!)
- 1 cup chocolate fudge
- Sprinkles

- Whipped cream
- 1 cup chopped nuts
- 1 cup cherries

· · · · · · · · · · · · · · **STEPS** · · · · · · · · · · · · · · ·

1. Place a small saucepan on the stove. Turn the stove on medium heat.

2. Pour the fudge into the saucepan. Heat the fudge until it is warm. Stir often.

3. While the fudge is warming, get your favorite ice cream from the freezer. Put three scoops into each bowl.

4. Once the fudge is warm, pour it over the ice cream.

5. Finish with your favorite toppings. Add sprinkles, chopped nuts, whipped cream, and top with a cherry.

6. Enjoy your ice cream sundae with friends!

Name: _____ Date: _____

Writing

Directions: Write the words from the Word Bank in alphabetical order. Then, choose three words, and write them in sentences. Be sure each sentence begins with a capital letter and ends with a punctuation mark.

Word Bank

baking	classes	quickly
replace	menu	poodle

Cumulative Review

Alphabetical Order

1. _____

2. _____

3. _____

4. _____

5. _____

6. _____

Sentences

1. _____

2. _____

3. _____

Standards Correlations

Shell Education is committed to producing educational materials that are research and standards based. To support this effort, this resource is correlated to the academic standards of all 50 states, the District of Columbia, the Department of Defense Dependent Schools, and the Canadian provinces. A correlation is also provided for key professional educational organizations.

To print a customized correlation report for your state, visit our website at **www.tcmpub.com/ administrators/correlations** and follow the online directions. If you require assistance in printing correlation reports, please contact the Customer Service Department at 1-800-858-7339.

Standards Overview

The Every Student Succeeds Act (ESSA) mandates that all states adopt challenging academic standards that help students meet the goal of college and career readiness. While many states already adopted academic standards prior to ESSA, the act continues to hold states accountable for detailed and comprehensive standards. Standards are designed to focus instruction and guide adoption of curricula. They define the knowledge, skills, and content students should acquire at each level. Standards are also used to develop standardized tests to evaluate students' academic progress. State standards are used in the development of our resources, so educators can be assured they meet state academic requirements.

College and Career Readiness

Today's college and career readiness (CCR) standards offer guidelines for preparing K–12 students with the knowledge and skills that are necessary to succeed in postsecondary job training and education. CCR standards include the Common Core State Standards as well as other state-adopted standards such as the Texas Essential Knowledge and Skills. The standards found on page 228 describe the content presented throughout the lessons.

TESOL and WIDA Standards

English language development standards are integrated within each lesson to enable English learners to work toward proficiency in English while learning content—developing the skills and confidence in listening, speaking, reading, and writing. The standards found in the digital resources describe the language objectives presented throughout the lessons.

Standards Correlations (cont.)

180 Days™: Phonics for Second Grade offers a full page of daily phonics practice activities for each day of the school year.

Every week provides practice activities tied to a variety of language arts standards, offering students the opportunity for regular practice in decoding, word recognition, phonics, reading, and writing.

Reading Foundation Skills
Know and apply grade-level phonics and word analysis skills in decoding words.
Distinguish long and short vowels when reading regularly spelled one-syllable words.
Know spelling-sound correspondences for additional common vowel teams.
Decode regularly spelled two-syllable words with long vowels.
Decode words with common prefixes and suffixes.
Identify words with inconsistent but common spelling-sound correspondences.
Recognize and read grade-appropriate irregularly spelled words.
Fluency
Read with sufficient accuracy and fluency to support comprehension.
Read grade-level text with purpose and understanding.
Use context to confirm or self-correct word recognition and understanding, rereading as necessary.
Range of Reading and Level of Text Complexity
By the end of the year, read and comprehend literature, including stories and poetry, in the grades 2–3 text complexity band proficiently, with scaffolding as needed at the high end of the range.
Writing
Recall information from experiences or gather information from provided sources to answer a question.

References Cited

Beck, Isabel L., and Mark E. Beck, 2013. *Making Sense of Phonics: The Hows and Whys, Second Edition.* New York: Guilford.

Marzano, Robert, 2010. "When Practice Makes Perfect Sense." *Educational Leadership* 68 (3): 81–83.

National Reading Panel, 2000. *Report of the National Reading Panel: Teaching Children to Read.* Report of the Subgroups Washington, DC: U.S. Department of Health and Human Services, National Institutes of Health.

Answer Key

There are many open-ended prompts and questions in this book. For those activities, answers will vary, and example answers are provided when possible.

Week 1

Overview (page 11)

m@t   s@n
p@t   t@p
p@g   v@t

Day 1 (page 12)

p@t b@g c@b f@n b@t
h@n t@p l@p j@g t@g
l@p r@t b@g j@t f@g
y@m p@n c@p w@g w@b
b@g h@g d@n t@p l@g

Day 2 (page 13)

a	pan, lap, ham, sat
e	pet, leg, neck, hen
i	kit, wig, hill, fin
o	tot, mop, fox, sob
u	bug, cut, buzz, tub

Day 3 (page 14)

pig pin pan ran rat
sun fun fan fat cat
mat map zap zip rip
hot hit bit bat bag
den pen pin tin tan

Day 4 (page 15)

1. mug   6. sun
2. dog   7. can
3. hot   8. gum
4. map   9. big
5. top   10. sit

Week 2

Overview (page 17)

c@nt   c@t   cit@
g@m   g@m

Day 1 (page 18)

Circle: gem, gel, cent, cereal
Box: gab, cot, cap, game

1. gem   5. gel
2. cot   6. game
3. cent   7. cap
4. gab   8. cereal

Day 2 (page 19)

soft c	cell, cent
hard c	cab, can, cop
soft g	gent, gem, gym
hard g	gap, got

Day 4 (page 21)

1. ice   5. cell
2. gem   6. germs
3. rice   7. gel
4. cent   8. gym

Day 5 (page 22)

1. gel   4. city
2. gym   5. cent
3. gem   6. cells

Week 3

Overview (page 23)

ship—/sh/ /ĭ/ /p/
chat—/ch/ /ă/ /t/
that—/th/ /ă/ /t/
whip—/wh/ /ĭ/ /p/
Phil—/ph/ /ĭ/ /l/

Day 1 (page 24)

1. ch / i / p   6. m / a / th
2. r / i / ch   7. wh / e / n
3. sh / i / p   8. wh / i / ch
4. m / a / sh   9. Ph / i / l
5. th / i / ck   10. g / r / a / ph

Day 2 (page 25)

/ch/	chop, chunk, chess
/sh/	shell, wish, shock
/th/	than, think
/wh/	wham, whip
/ph/	Ralph, graph

Day 3 (page 26)

Possible answers:

1. ship   6. chat
2. chin   7. bash
3. wish   8. thick
4. shop   9. when
5. math   10. sham

Day 4 (page 27)

1. chick   6. which, chess
2. shell
3. chop   7. Phil
4. thank   8. with
5. chit, chat   9. much, that
               10. bath

Day 5 (page 28)

1. chick   4. shell
2. graph   5. think
3. rich   6. which

Week 4

Overview (page 29)

knot   half   chalk
wrong   thumb

Day 1 (page 30)

wrong, chalk, half, knit, wrap, thumb, calf, numb, knob, wreck

Answer Key *(cont.)*

Day 2 (page 31)

wr–	wrong, wreck
–mb	thumb, numb
–lf	calf
kn–	knit, knot, knob
–lk	chalk, talk

Day 3 (page 32)

calf, thumb, half, knit, wrap, talk, lamb, write

1. wrap
2. calf
3. knit
4. talk
5. write
6. half
7. thumb
8. lamb

Day 4 (page 33)

wrong, wreck, wrap, limb, numb, knack, know, talk

Week 5

Overview (page 35)

s	n	i	p
s	t	o	p
s	w	i	m

Day 1 (page 36)

scuff step swing scan snack
spin stuck swam smell skin
snap stick scuff swim stuff
speck swat scab snug stop
skid smog smock sway stack

Day 2 (page 37)

sc–	scuff, scan, scab
sk–	skill, skin, skip
sm–	smell, smog
sn–	snap, sniff, snug
sp–	sped, spill
st–	still, stub
sw–	swing

Day 3 (page 38)

```
X M P V S K I N B E
K V V S S W V C D J S
S M V S I Y W S A Y G T
E T I C U Z N N Z N O
L F F F W Z C A E M R P
L F U C K H C K U B Y W
B U B H Y U U R D N Y
S K I L L E O B J Y S
T S T U C K J O X S
```

Day 4 (page 39)

Smith, skip, skill, best, swing, Steph, sniff, sticks, desk, smell

Day 5 (page 40)

1. smell
2. stem
3. skunk
4. swing
5. stuff
6. stack
7. spell
8. spin
9. stop
10. swim

Week 6

Overview (page 41)

click—/c/ /l/ /ĭ/ /k/
plum—/p/ /l/ /ŭ/ /m/
black—/b/ /l/ /ă/ /k/
slip—/s/ /l/ /ĭ/ /p/
glad—/g/ /l/ /ă/ /d/

1. click
2. plum
3. black
4. slip
5. glad

Day 1 (page 42)

clink, blend, plank, cloth, flock, floss, class, flag, glad, flash, sloth, slug, slack, glass, plum

Day 2 (page 43)

S Blends	scuff, stick, stop, swam, smell, snap, smog
L Blends	class, pluck, glad, clock, fluff, flesh, gloss, plum, glum

Day 3 (page 44)

bl–	cl–	fl–
blank	clam	flip
blip	cliff	fluff
blob	cluck	flash
blink	cloth	floss
gl–	pl–	sl–
glam	plum	slug
glad	plank	slick
gloss	pluck	sloth
glug	plan	sling

Day 4 (page 45)

1. sled
2. flag
3. flash
4. slam
5. glad
6. clock; class
7. plug
8. slush
9. glass
10. plan; floss

Week 7

Day 1 (page 48)

1. brick
2. frog
3. crop
4. drink
5. grass
6. truck

Day 2 (page 49)

S Blends	sniff, stem, swing, stuck, swam
L Blends	blink, club, cloth, glam, plank
R Blends	brick, trick, grip, cross, track, fresh

Day 3 (page 50)

Possible answers:

1. brick
2. grip
3. crack
4. grab
5. brink
6. bring
7. cram
8. brag

Day 4 (page 51)

frogs, grass, grip, fresh, traps, grab

Answer Key *(cont.)*

Day 5 (page 52)

1. bring
2. brunch
3. crash
4. grill
5. trick
6. truth

Week 8

Overview (page 53)

| s | p | l | a | sh |

| th | r | o | b |

Day 1 (page 54)

1. | sh | r | e | d |
2. | s | p | l | i | t |
3. | s | c | r | a | p |
4. | s | p | l | a | sh |
5. | sh | r | a | nk |
6. | th | r | a | sh |
7. | s | p | r | i | n | t |
8. | s | t | r | u | m |
9. | s | c | r | u | b |
10. | th | r | i | ll |

Day 2 (page 55)

Three-Letter Blends	scrub, strung, stress, sprint, splash, scratch, strum, sprang, scrap
Consonant Digraph Blends	shrank, shrill, throb, shrub, shred, thrill

Day 3 (page 56)

Down	Across
1. splash	2. sprint
4. shrink	3. scratch
5. spring	4. shrub
6. string	6. stress
7. shred	8. split

Day 4 (page 57)

Circle: instrument, stress, strap, strum, strings, throb, strong

Week 9

Day 1 (page 60)

ant   lump
blend   pest
bond   plump
cast   rant
chant   rent
chest   rest
clamp   shift
clump   sift
drift   spend
help   spent
kelp   vast
left   vest
lift   yelp

Day 2 (page 61)

–ft	gift, left, shift
–st	last, must, west
–lp	gulp, help, yelp
–nt	mint, spent, tent
–nd	blend, pond, sand
–mp	camp, lamp, ramp

Day 3 (page 62)

–ft	–st	–lp
gift	fast	kelp
raft	west	help
soft	last	yelp
lift	best	pulp

–nt	–nd	–mp
lent	land	lump
rent	band	damp
tent	sand	camp
lint	bend	pump

Day 4 (page 63)

1. sent
2. help
3. wind
4. twist
5. camp
6. help
7. pond
8. list
9. lent
10. lamp
11. loft
12. yelp

Day 5 (page 64)

1. blend
2. cast
3. clump
4. kelp
5. left
6. spent

Week 10

Overview (page 65)

blind   scold   most   bolt
child

Day 1 (page 66)

kind   wild   cold   post   jolt
bolt   told   child   mind   stall
ball   blind   molt   old   host
grind   mild   fold   gold   most
sold   wind   colt   rind   scold

Day 2 (page 67)

Closed Syllable Exceptions	grind, cold, post, bolt, blind, child, fall, pull
Closed Syllables	deck, swim, thin, gift, stop, which, thumb, wrath, knob

Day 3 (page 68)

```
I  J  J  E  T  E  T  M  G  W
S  T  A  L  L  K  V  N  O  I
K  J  L  N  N  I  B  G  L  L
C  J  A  S  C  O  L  D  D  D
F  H  V  L  F  I  N  D  C  J
O  Z  G  U  O  M  O  S  T  L
Y  F  N  R  P  U  L  L  N  L
T  P  X  Q  I  M  I  L  D  Y
X  T  M  O  A  N  B  O  L  T
O  P  D  D  I  G  D  L  Q  F
```

Day 4 (page 69)

child, gold, find, mind, wild, smile

Answer Key (cont.)

Day 5 (page 70)

1. gold
2. sold
3. cold
4. most
5. find
6. bolt
7. full
8. grind
9. ball
10. pull

Week 11

Overview (page 71)

pǎn	pāne
căp	cāpe
pǐn	pīne
cŭb	cūbe
nŏt	nōte

Day 1 (page 72)

cape   spice
safe   trace
wave   cage
chase   huge
whale   stage
dime   page
size   age
life   hose
vine   phone
hive   note
lace   close
mice   smoke
place

Day 2 (page 73)

| Short Vowels | clamp, scratch, stuck, shrub, crash, when, shock, twig, swam, stress |
| Long Vowels | time, space, cape, smoke, shape, rope, price, brake, crate, stripe |

Day 3 (page 74)

shine	**pine**	pipe	**stripe**	stride
ape	**grape**	grade	**wade**	wave
hole	hope	rope	ro**be**	gl**o**be
place	**sp**ace	spice	rice	ra**ce**
age	**c**age	**stage**	stake	st**o**ke

Day 4 (page 75)

Circle: Kate, likes, whale, love, same, make, made, waves, tide, close, name, Dave, here, came, huge, face

Week 12

Overview (page 77)

Circle: my, dry
Underline: lazy, tiny

Day 1 (page 78)

Long I: by, why, dry, cry, shy, sky, my, fly, style, type

Long E: spicy, lazy, lady, crazy, pricy, lacy, navy, shiny, tiny, cozy

Day 2 (page 79)

| Y as Long I | why, fry, by, my, shy, cry, sly, sky, fly, try |
| Y as Long E | spicy, navy, lady, crazy, shiny, candy, cozy, funny, happy, taffy |

Day 3 (page 80)

Day 4 (page 81)

1. baby, cry
2. shiny
3. Judy
4. why
5. my, candy
6. rainy, lazy
7. funny
8. taffy
9. lady
10. spicy

Day 5 (page 82)

1. fly
2. lady
3. shiny
4. shy
5. tiny
6. type

Week 13

Overview (page 83)

| s | ee | d |

| t | r | ea | t |

Day 1 (page 84)

1. | qu | ee | n |
2. | b | ea | ch |
3. | ch | ee | se |
4. | t | ea | ch |
5. | wh | ea | t |
6. | d | r | ea | m |
7. | s | l | ee | p |
8. | t | ee | th |
9. | ch | ee | r |
10. | p | ea | ch |

Day 2 (page 85)

| ee | feet, geese, queen, cheer, deep, tree, green, sweet, teeth |
| ea | meat, reach, bead, cheap, clean, leave, speak |

Day 3 (page 86)

Possible answers:

1. seen
2. peach
3. beach
4. sleep
5. lean
6. neat
7. beep
8. heal

Day 4 (page 87)

Highlight or circle: beach, feel, feet, cheek, please, see, each, sea, week, need, beep, freeze, cheer, reach

Week 14

Day 1 (page 90)

1. train
2. pay
3. paint
4. snail
5. clay
6. hay

Answer Key *(cont.)*

Day 2 (page 91)

ai	rainy, waist, hail, snail, drain, frail, raise, grain
ay	play, clay, hay, way, tray, sway, stray, gray

Day 4 (page 93)

Circle: rain, day, stay, wait, maybe

Underline: day, stay, wait, great

Week 15

Overview (page 95)

boat   grow   toe

Day 1 (page 96)

soap	toe	snow
mow	coat	yellow
pillow	road	foe

Day 2 (page 97)

oa	road, soap, float, coast, toast, coach, throat
ow	know, grow, window, show, pillow
oe	toe, doe, woe, Joe

Day 3 (page 98)

coat	**g**oat	**fl**oat	flat	fla**p**
low	**g**low	grow	**th**row	row
toe	**w**oe	w**all**	**b**all	**st**all
soak	soa**p**	sap	**cl**ap	clam
load	**r**oad	ro**d**	rod**e**	**r**ide

Day 4 (page 99)

groan, flows, Joan, window, slowly, snow, toes

Day 5 (page 100)

1. coat
2. throw
3. toe
4. know
5. goat
6. shadow
7. road
8. slowly
9. follow
10. oak

Week 16

Overview (page 101)

light high pie thigh lie tie

Day 1 (page 102)

high, pie, thigh, tie, flight, bright, lie, might, right, fight, night

Day 2 (page 103)

igh	tight, high, flight, might, night, sight, bright, thigh, slight, knight, sigh, fright
ie	die, lie, pie, tie

Day 3 (page 104)

Down	Across
1. tight	**2.** tie
3. light	**3.** right
4. flight	**4.** fight
6. pie	**5.** lie
	7. bright
	8. night

Day 4 (page 105)

Circle: high, night, flight, sight, delight

Highlight: high, sky, gleam, seem, glows, knows, smile, while, flight, sight, go, follow, night, delight, play, day

Week 17

Overview (page 107)

g	l	ue

h	oo	k

th	r	ew

b	oo	t

Day 1 (page 108)

hue clue glue blue true
spook booth hoop mood bloom
foot wood good hook shook
knew stew grew threw drew
look gloom blew flew dew

Day 2 (page 109)

ue	blue, glue
ew	blew, threw, stew, screw
/oo/ as in **book**	hood, cook, shook, book
/oo/ as in **moon**	droop, spook, bloom, troop, broom, zoom

Day 3 (page 110)

Possible answers:

1. flew
2. brew
3. clue
4. due
5. gloom
6. mood
7. cook
8. hood
9. wool
10. loop

Day 4 (page 111)

Circle: book, true, few, food, glue

Week 18

Overview (page 113)

d	aw	n

f	aw	n

h	au	l

Day 1 (page 114)

1. | h | au | l | | |
2. | f | l | aw | | |
3. | s | aw | | | |
4. | l | au | n | ch | |
5. | s | t | r | aw | |
6. | f | au | l | t | |
7. | c | r | aw | l | |
8. | v | au | l | t | |
9. | y | aw | n | | |
10. | sh | aw | l | | |

Answer Key *(cont.)*

Day 2 (page 115)

au	vault, launch, cause, fault, sauce, pause
aw	flaw, crawl, hawk, shawl, straw, yawn, paw, saw, draw, claw

Day 4 (page 117)

1. hawk
2. draw
3. claw
4. pause
5. sauce
6. crawl
7. straw
8. fault
9. saw
10. cause

Day 5 (page 118)

1. fault
2. hawk
3. launch
4. lawn
5. pause
6. straw

Week 19

Day 1 (page 120)

beach   snail   snow
night   pie   glue
draw   book   launch

Day 2 (page 121)

Long A ai/ay	play, tray, quail, train
Long E ee/ea	feet, week, meat, reach
Long I igh/ie	night, pie, flight, lie
Long O ao/ow/oe	goat, row, low, mow, boat
Long U ew/ue/oo	moon, true, dew

Day 3 (page 122)

```
Q U A I L   C Q U O   F
B  T Y F Z U  R J T U  A
S Q H G M  T T O W N  U
C O G F R R B H P W  L
O R S S E I D I R G  T
O C E O H W T Z H Q  M
P T R A I Z H O J    H
P  R U P A C P E E L R
B Y  E P W H B E B U C
Y    P T D L Z C M  C
```

Day 4 (page 123)

Circle: Reed, play, right, exclaims, feel, few, days, weeks, snow, freeze, seek, says, three, tree, hear, sound, peer, see, peach, peace, look, Joe, know, goes, great, team

Week 20

Day 1 (page 126)

1. | j | oy | |
2. | oi | n | k |
3. | b | oy | |
4. | oi | l | |
5. | j | oi | n |
6. | b | oi | l |
7. | f | oi | l |
8. | t | oy | |
9. | s | oi | l |
10. | c | oy | |

Day 2 (page 127)

oi	noise, oink, join, moist, voice, broil, coin, soil, point, boil
oy	toy, boy, joy, ploy, soy, enjoy

Day 3 (page 128)

Possible answers:

1. boy
2. boil
3. toy
4. loin
5. soy
6. soil
7. coin
8. coil

Day 4 (page 129)

oil, foil, broil, enjoy

Day 5 (page 130)

1. soil
2. foil
3. toy
4. choices
5. boy
6. enjoy
7. noise
8. coin
9. Boil
10. moist

Week 21

Day 1 (page 132)

1. cow
2. house
3. shout
4. clown
5. mouth
6. count

Day 2 (page 133)

ou	found, sour, count, mouse, sound, shout, pouch, loud, cloud, couch
ow	wow, crowd, plow, brow, cow

Day 4 (page 135)

sprout, doubt, wow, how, proud, cloud, found, ground, hound, snout, out

Week 22

Overview (page 137)

b	ar	n
th	or	n
p	er	ch

Answer Key (cont.)

Day 1 (page 138)

1. | sh | ar | k |
2. | m | ar | ch |
3. | h | ur | t |
4. | c | ur | l | y |
5. | s | qu | ir | t |
6. | ch | ir | p |
7. | n | or | th |
8. | s | t | or | m |
9. | s | c | ar | f |
10. | s | p | or | t |

Day 2 (page 139)

ar	dark, march, scarf, harp, star
er	fern, perch
ir	chirp, girl, squirt
or	north, sport, storm, thorn
ur	church, curb

Day 3 (page 140)

Down	Across
1. forty	2. chirp
3. hard	4. thorn
5. nurse	6. bark
6. burn	8. storm
7. verb	9. merge

Day 4 (page 141)

park, yard, warm, girls, soccer, sports, short, furry, perks

Day 5 (page 142)

1. chirp   4. perch
2. march   5. sport
3. north   6. storm

Week 23

Overview (page 143)

1. chair   4. glare
2. stare   5. hair
3. fair

Day 2 (page 145)

-air	air, fair, pair, hair, stair, repair
-are	stare, share, care, square, rare, scare, dare, snare, blare

Day 3 (page 146)

1. stair   6. pair
2. bare   7. fare
3. stair   8. stare
4. snare   9. chair
5. hair   10. blare

Day 4 (page 147)

1. hare   6. hair
2. fair   7. care
3. chair   8. air
4. stare   9. scare
5. glare   10. fairy

Week 24

Overview (page 149)

dear tear cheer fear steer

Day 1 (page 150)

1. deer   4. hear
2. steer   5. cheer
3. gear   6. clear

Day 2 (page 151)

-eer	steer, cheer, jeer, deer, sheer, sneer, veer
-ear	clear, year, dear, hear, gear, rear, spear, smear, fear

Day 3 (page 152)

jeer veer cheer chair pair tear dear deer sheer steer stair stare steer sneer snare spear smear hear hare dare square stare rare rear fear

Day 4 (page 153)

dear, cheer, gear, clear, rear, near, year

Day 5 (page 154)

1. cheer   6. shear
2. deer   7. clear
3. year   8. fear
4. near   9. Steer
5. beard   10. ears

Week 25

Overview (page 155)

store your sure pour more

Day 1 (page 156)

Circle in blue: court, your, four, mourn, pour

Circle in green: sore, chore, snore, store, wore, shore, score, ignore, before, explore, bore

Circle in red: pure, cure, injure, treasure

Day 2 (page 157)

-our	four, gourd, source, pour, course, mourn
-ore	score, explore, shore, more, chore, bore
-ure	cure, pure, ensure, injure

Day 3 (page 158)

Answer Key (cont.)

Day 4 (page 159)

sure, store, explore, shore, score, bore, ensure

Week 26

Overview (page 161)

1. lady; ladies
2. wishes
3. dogs
4. stops
5. catches
6. fly; flies

Day 2 (page 163)

1. bags
2. benches
3. classes
4. fries
5. stories
6. slides
7. trees
8. glasses
9. tables
10. spies
11. sheets
12. wishes

–s	bags, slides, trees, tables, sheets
–es	benches, classes, glasses, wishes
–ies	fries, stories, spies

Day 3 (page 164)

1. coat + s = coats
2. dish + es = dishes
3. light + s = lights
4. fly + ies = flies
5. catch + es = catches
6. fish + es = fishes
7. lady + ies = ladies
8. chair + s = chairs
9. story + ies = stories
10. baby + ies = babies

Day 4 (page 165)

butterflies, leaves, grasses, wings, flowers, eggs

Day 5 (page 166)

1. benches
2. blankets
3. dishes
4. glasses
5. stories
6. swings

Week 27

Overview (page 167)

1. fishing
2. skipping
3. raking
4. stopping
5. landing
6. hiding

Day 1 (page 168)

1. skip
2. hang
3. swing
4. run
5. bake
6. catch
7. hum
8. ride
9. make
10. write

Day 2 (page 169)

1. baking
2. catching
3. driving
4. ending
5. fading
6. pushing
7. ringing
8. running
9. skipping
10. writing

Add –ing	catching, ending, ringing, pushing
Double Final Consonant, Add –ing	running, skipping
Drop the e, Add –ing	baking, fading, driving, writing,

Day 3 (page 170)

1. writing
2. swinging
3. skipping
4. pushing
5. jumping
6. baking
7. making
8. running
9. driving
10. golfing

Day 4 (page 171)

Circle: growing, changing, sprouting, blooming, budding, flowering, stretching

Week 28

Overview (page 173)

1. acted
2. waved
3. stopped
4. loved
5. dumped
6. dropped

Day 1 (page 174)

1. /d/
2. /t/
3. /t/
4. /t/
5. /id/
6. /id/
7. /d/
8. /d/
9. /t/
10. /d/
11. /t/
12. /t/
13. /id/
14. /id/
15. /d/
16. /d/

Day 2 (page 175)

1. barked
2. biked
3. fished
4. handed
5. jotted
6. licked
7. lived
8. parked
9. sailed
10. zoomed

/t/	licked, barked
/d/	fished, biked, zoomed, parked, lived, sailed
/id/	jotted, handed

Day 3 (page 176)

1. rushed
2. tossed
3. boomed
4. rained
5. sailed
6. landed
7. jumped
8. rushed
9. waved
10. hiked

Day 4 (page 177)

Circle: enjoyed, played, zipped, zoomed, crashed, damaged, wanted, hoped, ended

Week 29

Overview (page 179)

nut/meg mag/net sub/tract sand/wich
VC/CV VC/CV VC/CCV VCC/CV

Answer Key *(cont.)*

Day 1 (page 180)

1. sun/set   VC/CV
2. rab/bit   VC/CV
3. mon/ster   VC/CCV
4. pen/cil   VC/CV
5. mush/room   VCC/CV
6. sud/den   VC/CV
7. kit/ten   VC/CV
8. hun/dred   VC/CCV
9. nap/kin   VC/CV
10. sub/tract   VC/CCV

Day 2 (page 181)

1. ath   lete
2. den   tist
3. gos   sip
4. dol   phin
5. hun   dred
6. in   sect
7. part   ner
8. sand   wich
9. ten   nis
10. trum   pet

VC/CV	insect, dentist, trumpet, gossip, tennis
VC/CCV	hundred, dolphin
VCC/CV	partner, sandwich, athlete

Day 3 (page 182)

sun**set**	in**sect**	**ham**ster
den**tist**	**ex**plode	chil**dren**
subtract	cac**tus**	
pumpkin	**kit**ten	

Day 4 (page 183)

1. rabbit
2. pencil
3. winter
4. dentist
5. pumpkin
6. doctor
7. birthday
8. insect
9. kitten
10. monsters

Day 5 (page 184)

1. monster
2. subtract
3. dolphin
4. trumpet
5. winter
6. letter
7. sunset
8. complete
9. conflict
10. bathroom

Week 30

Overview (page 185)

rob/in	sev/en
VC/V	VC/V
mel/on	fro/zen
VC/V	V/CV

Day 1 (page 186)

1. le/mon V/CV
2. ca/bin VC/V
3. ri/ver VC/V
4. pa/per V/CV
5. ro/bot V/CV
6. mu/sic V/CV
7. ti/ger V/CV
8. e/ven V/CV
9. ro/bin VC/V
10. pro/tect V/CV

Day 2 (page 187)

1. ba   sic
2. cab   in
3. di   ner
4. ho   tel
5. plan   et
6. pres   ent
7. riv   er
8. sal   ad
9. sec   ond
10. tal   ent

V/CV	basic, diner, hotel
VC/V	cabin, salad, talent, river, present, second, planet

Day 3 (page 188)

Down	Across
1. pilot	3. tulip
2. talent	5. open
4. robin	7. tiger
6. seven	9. even
8. lemon	10. hotel

Day 4 (page 189)

1. flut/ter
2. fall/ing
3. down/ward
4. soft/ly
5. emp/ty
6. re/main

Week 31

Overview (page 191)

rid/dle	an/gle
bot/tle	can/dle

Day 1 (page 192)

1. | j | u | n | g | le |
2. | a | pp | le | | |
3. | s | i | m | p | le |
4. | t | i | ck | le | |
5. | a | b | le | | |
6. | c | a | n | d | le |
7. | sh | u | ff | le | |
8. | p | ur | p | le | |
9. | c | r | u | m | p | le |
10. | t | ur | t | le | |

Day 2 (page 193)

Consonant +*le*	doodle, apple, giggle, snuggle, able, ripple, turtle, simple
Other Two-Syllable Words	robot, partner, second, seven, talent, penny, subway, railroad

Answer Key *(cont.)*

Day 3 (page 194)

Possible answers:

1. maple   5. cable
2. buckle   6. staple
3. pickle   7. settle
4. able   8. tumble

Day 4 (page 195)

1. buckle   6. waddles
2. doodle   7. jungle
3. purple   8. snuggle
4. apple   9. shuffle
5. candle   10. bottle

Day 5 (page 196)

1. candle   4. pickle
2. crumple   5. puzzle
3. jungle   6. table

Week 32

Overview (page 197)

unfair   impolite
unlucky   imperfect
untie   impossible

Day 1 (page 198)

1. uncap   to take cap off
2. unfair   not fair
3. impossible not possible
4. unclear   not clear
5. immature   not mature
6. imperfect   not perfect
7. impolite   not polite
8. impure   not pure
9. unfold   to not fold
10. unkind   not kind

Day 2 (page 199)

un–	unpack, unroll, untrue, unclear, untidy, unlike, unsafe, uneven, unlucky
im–	impolite, imperfect, impossible

Day 3 (page 200)

Day 4 (page 201)

untidy, unpack, unwind, unplug, unkind, unjust, impolite, uncap

Week 33

Overview (page 203)

recopy   dislike
remake   distrust
repack   displease

Day 1 (page 204)

1. recall   to think of something again
2. repack   to pack again
3. repay   to pay again
4. reread   to read again
5. retell   to tell again
6. dislike   to not like
7. distrust   to not trust
8. displace   to not place, to move
9. displease   to not please
10. distaste   to not taste, to not like

Day 2 (page 205)

to do again	repay, recycle, repack, rewind, rewrite, rewash, return, replace, reread
the opposite of	dislike, displease, distaste, discomfort, disobey, distrust

Day 3 (page 206)

1. recycle; to make something new again
2. rewrap; to wrap something again
3. rewrite; to write something again
4. dislike; to not like something
5. distrust; to not trust something
6. distaste; to not like something
7. repay; to pay again
8. rename; to name again
9. retell; to tell again

Day 4 (page 207)

1. discomfort   6. rewrap
2. displease   7. rewrite
3. reread   8. retype
4. reheat   9. discard
5. recopy

Week 34

Overview (page 209)

strongly   strong
easily   easy
strangely   strange
gladly   glad
hungrily   hungry

Day 1 (page 210)

1. proudly   6. quickly
2. gladly   7. loudly
3. happily   8. swiftly
4. slowly   9. quietly
5. lovely   10. easily

Answer Key (cont.)

Day 2 (page 211)

1. angrily
2. bravely
3. brightly
4. busily
5. calmly
6. happily
7. lonely
8. mostly
9. quickly
10. sloppily
11. strangely

–ly	calmly, bravely, strangely, quickly, brightly, lonely, mostly
Change y to i, Add –ly	angrily, sloppily, busily, happily

Day 3 (page 212)

Down:
1. gladly
2. quickly
3. neatly
4. kindly

Across:
5. gently
6. proudly
7. lovely
8. easily
9. loudly

Day 4 (page 213)

softly, gently, strongly, wildly

Day 5 (page 214)

1. easily
2. happily
3. quickly
4. quietly
5. sadly
6. slowly

Week 35

Overview (page 215)

1. can't
2. I'm
3. we're
4. it's

Day 1 (page 216)

1. I'm
2. he's
3. we're
4. isn't
5. I'll
6. they're
7. haven't
8. it's
9. aren't
10. hasn't

Day 2 (page 217)

Am	I'm
Are	they're, we're
Not	isn't, hasn't, shouldn't, don't, haven't, can't, weren't, aren't
Is	it's, he's, she's

Day 3 (page 218)

1. we're
2. haven't
3. isn't
4. it's
5. hasn't
6. I'm
7. he's
8. they're
9. aren't
10. she'll

Day 4 (page 219)

1. I'm; I am
2. Aren't; Are not
3. hasn't; has not
4. haven't; have not
5. didn't; did not
6. isn't; is not
7. can't; can not
8. He's: He is
9. They're; They are
10. We're; We are

Day 5 (page 220)

1. It's
2. He's
3. Isn't
4. aren't
5. I'm
6. We're
7. She's
8. hasn't
9. haven't
10. They're

Week 36

Overview (page 221)

p	ea	ch
s	t	ar	t
b	r	oi	l

Day 1 (page 222)

turtle   purse   dress
moose   splash   boy
child   ladies
bark   rainy

Day 2 (page 223)

R-Controlled Vowels	thorn, sport
Diphthongs	broil
Affixes	fixes, running, unfit, dislike, babies, repeal
Short Vowels	catch, knock, cent, thumb
Long Vowels	waist, thigh, stoke, paint, yellow, shadow, repeat

Day 3 (page 224)

spear   tear   team
gleam   gleams
lad   lamb   limb
climb   climbing
shell   fell   fill
spill   spilled
peach   peaches   beaches
reaches   roaches
sunshine   suntan   sunny
funny   funky

Day 5 (page 226)

1. baking
2. classes
3. menu
4. poodle
5. quickly
6. replace

Digital Resources

Accessing the Digital Resources

The digital resources can be downloaded by following these steps:

1. Go to **www.tcmpub.com/digital**

2. Use the 13-digit ISBN number to redeem the digital resources.

3. Respond to the question using the book.

4. Follow the prompts on the Content Cloud website to sign in or create a new account.

5. The content redeemed will appear on your My Content screen. Click on the product to look through the digital resources. All file resources are available for download. Select files can be previewed, opened, and shared.

For questions and assistance with your ISBN redemption, please contact Shell Education.

email: customerservice@tcmpub.com

phone: 800-858-7339

Contents of the Digital Resources

- Standards Correlations

- Class and Individual Analysis Sheets

- Fluency Rubric